James Goodwin Batterson

Gold and Silver as Currency in the Light of Experience,

Historical, Economical and Practical

James Goodwin Batterson

Gold and Silver as Currency in the Light of Experience, Historical, Economical and Practical

ISBN/EAN: 9783337253288

Printed in Europe, USA, Canada, Australia, Japan

Cover: Foto ©Suzi / pixelio.de

More available books at **www.hansebooks.com**

GOLD AND SILVER
AS CURRENCY

IN THE LIGHT OF EXPERIENCE, HISTORICAL
ECONOMICAL, AND PRACTICAL

❦❦❦

A Series of Papers

WRITTEN FOR THE TRAVELERS RECORD
BY
JAMES G. BATTERSON, President
OF
THE TRAVELERS INSURANCE COMPANY
HARTFORD, CONN.

❦❦❦

1896

❦❦❦

HARTFORD, CONN.
Press of The Case, Lockwood & Brainard Company
1896

GOLD AND SILVER

THE WORLD'S EXPERIENCE — ECONOMICAL, HISTORICAL, AND PRACTICAL.

THE economic questions of the day are a thousand times more important to the welfare of the people at large than any partisan interest which they may have in the distribution of political patronage. It is not the time for experiments with theoretical fancies which would set aside the experience of centuries; and it behooves every thinking man to cling to that which he knows to be practical, rather than follow those visionary schemes which can only promise success at the end of a rainbow.

The electric telegraph, swift ships, and modern inventions of every description have brought all nations so close together that we can no longer ignore the claim which each has upon the industries of the other. The products of American industry are everywhere to be found, and the United States is a large consumer of the products of all other countries. This universal barter, which is the distribution of the surplus abundance of one country for that of another, makes up the principal volume of the world's commerce, and is the great force in the civilization of mankind. The productions comprised in this universal barter or exchange have all to be weighed and measured in order that justice may everywhere be done. There is as yet no universal standard either of weights or measures, but the standards of each country are within very small limits convertible into the standards of all. The adjustment of the final balance in all transactions of barter is by a payment in coin which measures the difference in values at the point where the exchange is made.

3

The division of labor, also, not only between the states and the peoples of a single country, but between the nations of the earth, is the highest type of universal civilization. The exchange of products, skilled labor, and inventions being the substance of commerce, is the bond of social intercourse both at home and abroad. Every impediment in the way of building up our own commerce and extending our trade with other nations is a hindrance to the progress of civilization and a hindrance to the payment of our just debts, which can only be paid with our own products and the thrift of our own people. England, France, Germany, and Holland have purchased our securities with gold: we cannot legislate their payment in silver. By the full amount of our foreign indebtedness, we are now under bonds to preserve a gold basis with those countries, and we cannot change it until we pay our debts, and then we will not want to. Destroying our credit is a very poor way to pay debts.

Before the Civil War "cotton was king," and supplied a larger volume of exchange on London than any other product in this country. When the writer was in Egypt in 1859 cotton was a very scarce commodity in the port of Alexandria; now every mill in New England and old England buys Egyptian cotton, and cheap labor in the valley of the Nile and in India affects the great staple of our Southern States unfavorably. We cannot prohibit its importation without promoting increased cultivation in Egypt and India. The Soudan is the natural cotton country of the world, and it is larger than the United States. England has long been reaching out for that prize and will get it soon.

These economic questions cannot be controlled by legislation, any more than we can force the cultivation of tea and coffee in Colorado and Montana. The silver miners in those States get from $3.50 to $4.00 per day for their labor; the Egyptian fellaheen are content to raise cotton for a mere fraction of such wages, where food, shelter, and clothing cost little, and being deprived of the last would not cause them to suffer.

The world's supply of cotton is so large that the foreign demand on the Southern States has fallen off, and this great industry of our country has suffered seriously in consequence. Cultivators of wheat, corn, and tobacco, with all other industries, have experienced the same loss of demand for their products, and the values have been greatly diminished.

The silver producing States have had a like experience in loss of demand for their product, but they now ask their sister States to join them in creating such an artificial demand for the silver product as will give it an advantage over all other products, which in turn would reap no corresponding benefit, but on the contrary would find the gain to silver an additional burden to themselves.

The theory that silver can be coined into money, and that the mint stamp can arbitrarily fix its value, and thereby make money plenty for everybody, is founded on the theory proposed for the relief of all who are suffering, not from any "scarcity of money," but a diminished demand for their products.

The fallacy of attempting to *create* an additional value by the mere stamp of the mint is demonstrated by the fact that the present difference between the nominal value of the silver dollar coined under the acts of 1878 and 1890, and the market value of the same as bullion, is just about $200,000,000 which the people at large have had to pay or must pay, as the measure of relief already given to the producers of silver in this country. The same proportionate expenditure for sustaining the prices of cotton, wheat, corn, tobacco, and potatoes would have bankrupted the government. The citizen who digs potatoes and the citizen who digs for silver should have the same measure of protection, or both should be left to the natural laws of supply and demand.

Further demonstration, if needed, is found in the historical and practical experience of all countries and all ages with the commercial relations of

GOLD AND SILVER COINAGE.

Both of the metals named, when extracted from their native ores and remaining in bulk, are termed *bullion*. After refinement and admixture with the legal proportion of alloy to secure hardness, it is called *standard bullion*.

Charlemagne was the first to establish a pound weight of silver as the unit of value. The same unit was subsequently adopted by England, France, and Italy, and it became by its multiples and sub-multiples the foundation of the English nomenclature, pounds, shillings, and pence, and assumed the function of money as a convenient measure of value in exchange for all other commodities. The single pound of standard bullion, divided into twenty equal parts, made twenty shilling pieces, each weighing one-twentieth of a pound. Divided into four pieces, each weighing one-quarter of a pound, they were called crowns. Two shillings sixpence was half a crown, a sixpenny piece weighed six two-hundred-and-fortieths of a pound, or a pound divided into forty equal parts.

Edward I. changed the ratios slightly by coining 243 pence out of the silver pound. Up to the time of Elizabeth repeated changes had been made until they reached 744 pence to the pound of silver, making sixty-two light shillings where there was only twenty by the original standard.

During the reign of Charles II. the English African Company sent home a large quantity of gold from the coast of Guinea. Charles coined this gold into pieces which he called *guineas*, and were intended to conveniently represent the silver pound in value. By the bullion values in the markets of different countries it was found that the guinea was worth 20s. 8d. as compared with the relative value of a pound of silver; but the government declared it to have the *current* value of twenty-one shillings silver, and both gold and silver were made legal tenders to any amount. For this reason debts could be paid more profitably in gold than silver, as it had a legal tender value of 4d. in the pound over silver, which being depressed at home was sent abroad, under the operation of Gresham's economic law.

In 1816 gold was declared to be the only measure of value to an unlimited amount, and the gold sovereign was struck to represent the value of twenty shillings in silver, or the pound unit. This gave silver an artificial value of about six per cent., and was likely to drive the new sovereign out of circulation, but the mischief was averted by limiting the legal tender in silver to forty shillings.

Aristophanes was the first to discover that a base or depreciated coinage always remained in circulation, while the better coins immediately disappeared from the markets. The same fact has been noticed by careful observers ever since, and it has become a well-settled economic law. The reason is obvious: if coins of full weight and value are allowed to circulate with those which are depreciated, the bad will remain and the good will disappear; for every one will try to pay his debt with the depreciated coin, while those of full weight will go to the money-changers in exchange for coins of the same legal value but of less real value, and thus make a profit by withdrawing the best currency from circulation.

The United States trade dollar, which was 7½ grains heavier than the ordinary dollar, was coined for international circulation. The ordinary or light dollar was a legal tender, but the trade dollar was not; the consequence was, the trade dollars were all exported and never came back, being worth more as bullion than as dollars.

In this connection the variable character of the ratios at different historical periods is worthy of attention. Herodotus gives it as 1 to 13, Plato 1 to 12, Menander 1 to 10, and in Cæsar's time it was 1 to 9. From 1663 to 1717 silver was the standard of value in England, and gold passed at its market value only, but the guinea was sometimes rated at thirty shillings silver. After the re-coinage in 1696 the guinea stood at 21s. 6d. Sir Isaac Newton, who was master of the mint, proposed to reduce the guinea to a circulating value of 21s. At a parity with silver it should have been 20s. 8d. Remaining at 21s., a difference of only four pence to the pound, drove out the white metal, and England was forced to a gold currency. The opposite treatment in France gave that country a silver currency, and the silver standard prevailed. On the other hand, the discovery of gold in California and Australia added so immensely to the stock of the world's gold that the ratios were changed by their new conditions ; the fundamental law before referred to asserted itself, and the currency of France became gold in place of silver.

Such fluctuations as we have quoted under a double standard cannot be prevented by the combined power of all nations. An international congress cannot suspend the laws of gravitation. No bimetallic ratio of 16 to 1 or 30 to 1 can prevent one or the other from having its value as bullion, regardless of its stamp at the mint, which determines nothing but the quality and quantity of the bullion in the coin.

An act of Congress may make one metal or the other or both a legal tender for debts, and thereby create a fictitious value; but with a very slight change of the ratio in market values, one or the other will be sold as bullion, and that which remains for a circulating medium will always be the least valuable as bullion. Such is the immutable law which has governed this question in all ages, and no power on earth can change it.

What is the best course for this country to pursue for the advancement of its permanent prosperity, is a matter of judgment, but the facts of history are the common property of mankind and the true guides to wisdom for the formation and exercise of a sound judgment.

EXCHANGE.

The artificial impediments created by different systems of coinage in various countries having commercial intercourse are regulated and adjusted by the nominal rate of exchanging the coinage of one country for that of another.

The gold coinage of England has twenty-two carats pure metal to two carats alloy, each coin having a percentage of 8.33+ alloy. If the United States coinage is below this standard, and has only twenty or twenty-one carats pure metal to three or four carats alloy, we cannot exchange it for English coin of the same weight without paying the difference in value, which difference is the fixed nominal *exchange*. When the two countries have the same standard for coinage, then the exchange is reckoned at par. If however, they use different metals, gold and silver, there can be no such thing as par of exchange, because the relative market value is constantly changing.

COMMERCIAL EXCHANGE.

When the bankers in London and New York owe each other equal amounts, the debts of one offset the other, and the accounts being balanced no money passes. If, however, on settling day New York owes London one or two or three millions the most, then the balance of trade is against us, and we must pay the difference in coin. During this condition of trade bankers' bills and commercial bills drawn against bank credits, shipments of corn, cotton, wheat, silver, or any other product, will sell at a premium, because they are payable in gold of the highest standard and at a foreign port. This premium, it will be seen, can never exceed the *specie point*, which is the cost of shipping gold from New York to London or *vice versa*, which, with insurance and carriage, is reckoned at about $5,000 for each million shipped, and is the cost of maintaining such commercial transactions on a specie basis. So, also, when the balance of trade is in our favor, London exchange will be at a discount; but that discount can never fall below the cost of shipping gold from London to New York. The two specie points of premium and discount, therefore, mark the extreme limits of commercial exchange between these two great countries, because when the limit is reached the gold will be shipped one way or the other as the balance may be.

The rate of interest at different points also affects the movement of gold. If the Bank of England will lend its surplus gold at two per cent. and New York will pay six per cent., the London bankers will ship gold to New York and meet the demand; but when the surplus is being reduced towards the point fixed for the reserve, then the bank raises the rate of interest and stops the outward flow of its gold by making the shipment abroad unprofitable. So it is also with wheat, cotton, or any other commodity. When the demand is great and the price is high in England, large shipments will be made from America until the English price falls so as to make further shipments unprofitable.

A depreciated currency necessarily creates an adverse condition of the market for exchange and destroys credit. All history shows that there is no cure for the evil but a prompt return to sound conditions.

Gold naturally flows to the cheapest point for the purchase of commodities, and is borne thither by enterprising traders who find their best profits in the most abundant and cheapest markets.

VALUE.

While gold has been selected as the most stable *measure* of value in exchange, so *demand* has always pre-determined the value of commodities to be measured for exchange or commercial distribution. Any commodity for which there is no demand has no value. Gold as the standard of measure is constant : but the *demand* for commodities is subject to great fluctuations. The only commodity for which there is no limit to the demand must always be the best standard of measure for all other commodities.

When the law arbitrarily fixes the equation of 16 to 1 for silver and gold, the people will experience very serious trouble when the commercial ratios are at variance with the law. For example, the law declares that in payment of debts sixteen ounces of silver shall be received as the equivalent for one ounce of gold ; but if the debtor or buyer has gold, or a gold credit, he will never use it in payment of his debt, for with the ounce of gold he can under some conditions buy thirty ounces of silver, pay his debt with sixteen ounces, and have fourteen ounces of silver left, making a saving of 47 per cent. on his debt. It will be observed, however, that the possessor of gold is the only one who can

make this saving; for he who has only silver cannot buy the
gold without a loss in silver which is fully equal to the
amount saved in paying his debt. English traders who deal
so largely in American products, will first buy silver with
their gold, and pay it to the planter for his cotton, and the
farmer for his wheat, the effect of which would be to export
gold and import silver where there is enough already.

It will be claimed, however, that the *demand* for silver
will be so great that in the course of time these abnormal
conditions will disappear by reason of a readjustment of
prices; but when India and Egypt with their cheap labor
control the price of cotton, and Russia, India, and the Argentine Republic control the price of wheat in Liverpool,
we shall have these and similar external difficulties to overcome, and the road to readjustment will be long and diffi-
cult.

The holders of $9,000,000,000 of obligations in the form
of life insurance policies will not be made happy if they are
paid in silver or any other depreciated currency; and yet if
the premiums are to be paid in silver, the policies will have
to be paid in the same coin.

If the merchant who has insured his goods against de-
struction by fire on a gold value, can only collect his damage
in silver, whenever it is made a legal tender, he will suffer
largely thereby ; and this applies to every man's house or
business building in the country as the immediate effect of
a loss by fire, unless the policies are re-written to fit the
changed conditions.

The adoption of a bimetallic currency on the basis of 16
to 1, making both metals a legal tender for debts, every
thoughtful man must know will lead us into silver monometallism and multiply the evils from which we would
escape.

Congress has no power to fix the value of any commodity, except as a *legal tender ;* and when this legal value is
above the world's markets it is purely fictitious, but it will
pay any man's debt who has something he can exchange for
it, but which does not possess an equal debt-paying power as

legal tender. The difference between the purchasing power of gold and silver is evidenced by the premium on gold, which is only another expression for the discount or diminution in the relative value of silver, but does not necessarily signify a relative increase in the value of gold. So the term "scarcity of money" does not mean that there is really any less money than before, but that the condition of trade invites its employment and circulation in business affairs. A "tight money market" generally means that the banks have been drained by the demands of an active business, and the rate of interest is high.

INVESTMENTS.

Savings banks, trust companies, insurance companies, estates, and private persons hold an enormous volume of bonds issued by States, counties, towns, railroad and other corporations, payable principal and interest in gold; such being the contract when the bonds were sold, and the price and rate of interest were then adjusted to that basis. Now if Congress, the supreme law-making power, shall enact that silver on the basis of 16 to 1 of its weight with gold shall be a legal tender for "*all debts*" and for "*all amounts,*" it may be very serious, unless the contract shall take precedence, and render the legal tender act inoperative as to this most important class of securities, for otherwise they would decline in value more than fifty per cent., and the distress and indignation of the people would rise superior to that of any power which could so mistake its duty to the public. Hundreds of millions have been added to the public debt in the vain endeavor to legislate a parity of silver with gold on a basis which is not only arbitrary but impossible. There is no more reason for governmental bounties on the production of sugar and silver than there is on cotton and wheat. The decline in the price of these products has been greater than the decline in the price of silver, and the distress has been very great. We seem to forget that the products of the United States are not a national monopoly; all the nations of the earth are in sharp competition with us, and the laws of supply and demand will everywhere prevail without respect to the acts of Congress.

Natural laws are adjusted to changing conditions automatically. The closer we observe and the closer we keep to natural conditions the better it will be, and the nearer we shall come to an automatic adjustment of our currency with the affairs of the people.

William the Conqueror put one-twentieth of a pound weight of silver into his shilling. Elizabeth only one-third as much, but William's shilling would buy as much bread as three of Elizabeth's. We must either put a dollar's worth of silver in a silver dollar, or the farmer will have to change the size of his bushel and the merchant his yard-stick so as to be on equality with the measure of silver. If silver is not given a fictitious value as a legal tender, silver dollars will then pass at their real value in exchange for wheat or payment of debts. Make the legal tender value and the bullion value alike, and it will wrong no one. Free coinage will then do no harm and honest dollars will multiply automatically to fill the demands of trade.

If these historical facts are worth anything as guides to the future, then it is certainly true that the United States government cannot maintain the world's volume of silver at parity with gold, on the basis of 16 to 1, without bankruptcy.

The demand for a silver standard, about 1,100 years ago, was a long step forward. The demand for it now is a long step backward.

To say that the millions of savings bank depositors, who are mostly poor people, may be paid off with dollars worth only fifty-three cents, would be an ugly item in our financial history.

The bimetallic scheme for reducing the purchasing power of the laborer's wages fifty per cent. will not go unchallenged in the workshops and fields.

The theory that unlimited coinage of silver with an unlimited legal tender, will be a great relief to the debtor, is unwittingly a confession of its iniquity. The debts which one man owes, another man owns. A poor man sells his farm because he lacks the means or the health to work it; his more thrifty neighbor buys it and executes a mortgage for payment upon the interest of which the poor man must live. By what principle of equity must the poor man be robbed of half his bread, in order that the thrifty buyer of his land may get it at half the price he agreed to pay? From the standpoint of commercial honesty this doctrine is wrong end up.

The railway indebtedness of this country is the largest of all; said to be over $6,000,000,000. It is owned everywhere, at home and abroad, and interest and principal is largely payable in gold; making the income payable in silver would double the debt and bankrupt the companies, filling the land with beggars and relieving neither the one who owes, nor the one who owns.

We may pump indefinitely the waters of the sea into capacious cisterns, but we cannot change its level. One Congress after another may force the purchase of silver by the sale of gold-bearing bonds, and bankrupt the treasury; while its vaults are filled to repletion, not a grain will thereby be added to or taken from the world's stock of bullion, and the government "*fiat*" will be the jest of mankind.

PROTECTION.

The most extravagant protectionist has never presumed to ask the government to "*fiat*" his product and then make the fiat good by selling bonds and purchasing the wares which the markets will not take. That sort of protection feeds upon its own vitals, and is of short duration.

INTRINSIC VALUE.

Very many people have an idea that silver has an *intrinsic* value which does not pertain to other commodities. From an economic standpoint, however, it has been well established that the value of any commodity is to be judged by its relation to other commodities entirely extraneous to itself and for which it may be exchanged.

The term *intrinsic* must necessarily refer to a quality within itself and not to anything external. Any commodity, therefore, which has no subject of comparison other than itself cannot be said to have a definite value in an economic sense. The value of use may have its effect on the value of exchange, but in economics there can be no other value than that of exchange, and the value of use is not considered; neither is the amount nor cost of the labor required to produce it. It may cost double to produce a given quantity of silver from low grade ores in one State than it costs under more favorable conditions in another; but that fact has no consideration in the bullion market. A Bank of England note which will exchange for gold has an economic value but no intrinsic value, and the labor of its production is not considered. The concurrent demand for two commodities in diff_rent possession, is the original source of value and the cause of exchange, which, being common to all commodities, determines the relation of one to the other, and gives a definition of value which is natural and consistent.

ARTIFICIAL VALUES.

Artificial values are created by excessive and unnatural demands. Congress may arbitrarily order the purchase of three or four millions of silver per month and coin it into dollars, for which there is no other need or demand than the desire of the producer to sell; but the time comes when it has to stop, and the reaction is more disastrous to commercial affairs than the entire value of the silver purchased.

The stock of silver owned and controlled by the United States government is a menace to the whole world, and has done the silver-producing states more harm than it is all worth. Stimulating production at extravagant cost in order to take advantage of a forced, arbitrary, and unnatural demand must always be ruinous when the time comes for restoration to the natural order of all things.

THE UNIT.

The unit of value in the United States is twenty-five and eight-tenths grains of gold nine-tenths fine ; and this quantity and quality is called a dollar. Its principal use is the service which it renders as the standard measure of all other commodities for which it may be exchanged. The selection of this material for the office which it performs is the result of an experience in trade which covers the entire history of civilization, and the experiments and practice of mankind in all nations with divers other substances and things as substitutes and legal equivalents, the chief of which is silver.

Gold and silver have been termed the precious metals, for the reason that they have useful and desirable properties other than the money value of exchange. Their intrinsic *qualities* are imperishable and unchangeable. Pure gold and silver have but one quality of metal, and there are no adjectives like good, better, and best to describe such quality. They have great utility in the arts, and being indestructible are most desirable for possession, and take high rank in the confidence of all men as security for debt and a certificate of credit for the prompt supply of all needful commodities. The selection of these metals to perform the functions of money has been the natural development of the ages, and is witness to the universal judgment of all nations that they are best qualified for that service. So long as the supply and demand kept the two metals on a natural parity, it was only a matter of convenience or choice whether it should be one pound of gold or sixteen pounds of silver ; but when the markets are everywhere overstocked with silver, and the pressure to sell is greater than the demand, then the parity is lost, confidence disturbed, and it is utterly repudiated as a standard of measure, except to that extent which the law compels its reception for debt. For this disastrous condition of things there is only one remedy, and that is to *stop production until the natural parity is restored.* Passing laws to restore parity at the cost of the public treasury would only be another name for a charge or tax on all other commodities for the amount required. This would stimulate further production, multiply the evil, destroy confidence, and make the crash all the more terrible by its postponement, at the cost of national credit.

If silver has been demonetized, who in the wide world is responsible for it but the silver producers who have so choked the bullion markets of the world that the demand has been smothered by an over supply. The very fact that the vaults of the United States Government are all full and can hold no more is a constant hazard to the bullion markets of the world. The German government relieved its own surcharged vaults by selling its silver for so much gold as they could get for it. It was a relief to Germany, but a load on the general market. The United States Government cannot now sell its stock of silver for one-half its original cost. The silver producers now propose to relieve themselves by such legislation as will force all other industries to buy the product at a higher price than it is worth in any market in the world, for they tell us that this forced demand would put up the price of bullion, and increase the purchasing power of the silver dollar. What reason in the world the farmer can have for putting up the price of silver, when by the same act he is forced to buy it with a larger quantity of wheat, does not appear; as the price of wheat is governed by the market in Liverpool, and the farmer cannot mark up his wheat to meet the price of silver. It is for the interest of all industries that they be allowed to buy silver dollars if they want them on the best terms possible, and without any interference on the part of government in the interest of silver at the people's expense.

The claim that free coinage and unlimited tender would make money plenty for every man's use is squarely against the experience of ages and opposed to well-known principles of economic science. If it is true that the price of silver would rise by reason of the unnatural pressure of law and artificial demand, it cannot possibly be true that the price of wheat and cotton would be higher in the same proportion, for Russia, India, Egypt, and the Argentine Republic control the price of wheat and cotton in this country by making the price in Liverpool ; and this cannot be prevented by acts of Congress, neither by the rise or fall of silver.

Bimetallism means a double standard, two metals both of which being declared by Congress to have a fixed relative and nominal value, and either may be taken at its nominal value as the true measure of all other values in exchange ; but in payment of debts the debtor *may take his choice which metal he will use*, and he always uses that which has the lowest market or exchange value. Quick to perceive the effect of the double standard, the seller now *takes his option* and *marks up his goods* to a point where opposite the dollar-mark we read fifty per cent. discount for payment in gold and no credit. He has discovered that a *measure* which is at one time four per cent. too long and at another is fifty per cent. too short, is not much of a *standard* for anything. He has also found an economic truth that there can be only one standard and that exactness in the measure of values in use and values in exchange, does not reside permanently in anything.

The advocates of bimetallism and a double standard contend, that the differences referred to do not show a decline in the exchange value of silver, but a rise in the exchange value of gold. If this claim is true, how can it be demonstrated so that the fact may be considered proven and no longer left open as an item in the dispute ?

From 1860 to 1873 it is certain that silver commanded a premium over the gold standard continuously from one to four per cent., and for that reason disappeared entirely from circulation, and fractional paper currency took its place. During the year 1873 the decline in silver reached its parity with gold.

The average price per fine ounce in 1873 was $1.28.24.

The average value of the silver dollar in 1873 was .98.87.

The commercial ratio of silver to gold in 1873 was 16.17 to 1.

The average price per fine ounce in 1893 was .70.17.

The average value of the silver dollar in 1893 was .54.27.

The commercial ratio of silver to gold in 1893 was 29.45 to 1.

The same corresponding values and ratios prevailed in the exchanges of Europe.

This enormous decline over a period of twenty years is to be accounted for so that we can determine whether it is to be attributed to a rise in gold, or fall in silver, and the question should be met fairly.

First. In 1873 the world's production of silver for the year was $81,800,000.

Year by year the rate of production increased until it reached in 1892 an annual production of $196,105,000, an increase of more than 239 per cent. over the year 1873, when silver was par with gold.

Second. In 1873 Germany adopted the single gold standard, and threw upon the bullion markets of Europe her large stock of silver, which caused a sharp decline.

Third. In 1873-4-5 Denmark, Norway, Sweden, and Holland adopted the gold standard and stopped the coinage of silver except for small change.

Fourth. In 1878 the Latin Union stopped the coinage of full legal tender silver coins and it has not been resumed.

Fifth. In 1876 Russia suspended the coinage of silver except for such amounts as were required for her trade with China.

Sixth. In 1879 Austria, and in 1892 Hungary, suspended the free coinage of silver, and adopted the gold standard.

Seventh. In 1893 India closed her mints to free coinage, and the United States repealed the purchasing clause of the act of 1890, which called for 4,500,000 ounces per month.

There was nothing to prevent the declination of silver, which simply obeyed the laws of gravitation, and it was excessive production more than all other causes combined which forced it down. An increase of the supply and a decrease in the demand, produced its natural result.

In this connection it would be unwise to say that the increased demand for gold in those countries where it had been made the single standard did not have any effect upon the exchange value of gold for other commodities. But as it has been made *the standard* by which all other values are measured, there is no other "bench-mark" or fixed point, above or below which the fluctuations, if any, can be measured as to its own value in exchange, therefore such standard measure or unit of value must be treated as constant and invariable for economic questions. Every attempt to erect another standard by which the constancy of the gold standard shall be tried, will only result in confusion, and disturb rather than create confidence in any standard.

There are but three options : The single gold standard, the bimetallic or double standard, and the single silver standard.

To the single gold standard, the objection is raised that there is not gold enough in the world for that purpose, and in all fairness it must be admitted, that if all nations should suddenly adopt the single gold standard the strain at certain points would be very great, and for a time considerable inconvenience would follow. Those countries would suffer the most where the people are their own bankers and everything bought is paid for in cash from hand to hand.

Banks are the natural and convenient clearing-houses for the people ; and where they exist under proper regulations and restrictions the actual volume of cash required by the community which they serve is only a fraction of that which would otherwise be an absolute necessity. A check for one thousand dollars may transfer a bank credit from A. to B., and again from B. to C., and C. to D., until the actual trade liquidations of that one payment may amount to ten, twenty, or thirty thousand dollars, without the handling of a single specie dollar. This is illustrated on a large scale by the daily bank clearings in the city of New York. The day would not be long enough and the risk would be very great for each bank to collect the checks which in a single day's business are received over its counter on many other city banks ; whereas, by sending them all into the clearing-house the exchanges are made in an hour, and the balance only has to be provided for, which is but a mere fraction of the business transacted. So, also, between commercial nations the exchanges are made by bills of exchange, drafts, letters of credit, etc., and coin is only shipped to cover balances which are comparatively small. But a single gold standard would not prevent the use of silver in moderate transactions, nor for purposes of change. If its legal-tender value is limited to ten dollars *there will be no less silver in active circulation than there is now.*

A bimetallic or double standard is an utterly impossible thing; two weights for a standard pound, two lengths for a standard yard, are gross absurdities.

The third option is a single silver standard, by means of which gold would become a commodity, with its central market in London, and none in the United States, for it would all leave us.

The strong reasons in favor of a single silver standard are : —

First. It is one of the great products of the country, and we want to sell it. In this respect it occupies the same position as wheat, corn, cotton, tobacco, and all other products, the surplus of which we are compelled to sell at the market price, whatever it may be. The silver farmer cannot sell his crop in Europe because the markets are overstocked and the price is low, therefore he goes to Congress and asks the government to buy his product and take the risk of holding it. This gives the silver producer an advantage which no other producer enjoys, and is unfair to every other industry which takes the risk of its own production.

Second. "If silver is made the *standard* measure of all values in this country then the demand for its use as money would be so largely increased that the price would go up immediately to par with gold," which means an advance of 50 per cent. in the price of silver.

If that is true, then the cotton planter, and the wheat raiser, would have to pay in their products double price for their dollars, because the government cannot use its power to put up the price of wheat and cotton as well as silver. It will be observed that the plan for a silver standard means also that the silver producer can exchange his surplus product for gold, while all other industries must exchange their surplus products for silver. The silver producer does not care to exchange silver for silver, unless the silver he gets in return is made a *legal tender* for all amounts — and in that condition he can exchange it for gold.

It is a great fallacy, however, to suppose that the increased use of silver for currency will materially advance the price unless all other nations adopt the same standard, for it is certain that even a small advance in the price would bring to the United States a sufficient supply from Europe to force it down again.

FREE COINAGE.

Will do no harm unless silver is made a legal-tender for all amounts ; limit the legal-tender to ten dollars and no one will waste breath on free coinage.

Nothing can be permanent which gives any one product an unjust advantage over all other products at government expense. It is purely a question of economics and just trade, and not a question of party politics.

The cry for "*cheap money* and *plenty of it*," is a catch phrase, and a bait to the unwary. When business is good, good money abounds. When business is bad, bad money does not make it better. The laborer cannot obtain even bad money for idleness ; but when his labor is in demand he has no trouble in getting the best.

The treasury vaults in Washington and elsewhere are filled with silver until there is no room for more, but it does not promote business.

The government is issuing bonds and buying gold to maintain the parity of idle silver, and stimulate the production of more, but it does not stimulate business nor inspire confidence either at home or abroad. It is a policy in direct opposition to the experience of the ages, and the best authorities the world over condemn it. The drastic remedy for an over-production of tenantless houses is to *stop building*. If on the contrary a booming city government in order to provide employment for its idle masons and carpenters sells bonds, lays out new streets, and continues to build, it involves the whole community in a general bankruptcy, and the remedy is worse than the disease. Buying four hundred millions of silver gave temporary relief to the miners, and a lasting burden to the people. It did not stop the decline, but hastened it by continued production. The extra session of 1893 stopped further buying, but the stock now piled up in the government vaults could not be quickly sold for more than one-third its cost. Such is the result of applying artificial force to the natural laws of supply and demand.

LIFE INSURANCE AND SAVINGS BANKS.

The advocates of a silver standard have severely condemned the officers of those companies which have given warning that a silver standard with a silver deposit and a silver premium will bring forth nothing but silver. By thus rejecting the natural crop from the seed they sow, they condemn themselves. They are, indeed, of those who would gather grapes from thorns, and figs from thistles. The people's reserve for the future is largely with life insurance companies and savings banks. The resulting possibilities are the effects of accumulating compound interest. If this accumulation is silver then the dividends and payments must be silver, and the officers and directors of these companies have no power to do otherwise, for whatsoever is sown that they must reap, and of all men the advocates of a silver standard should not reject the fruit from their own planting. Nothing can be more significant of the danger which lurks in this scheme than the bad temper with which its advocates have received the suggestion that they may, some day, have to accept their own coin in payment of their own claims.

WANT OF CONFIDENCE.

England takes first rank as a commercial power because of the integrity and stability of her monetary system. The pound-sterling is known and respected at its true value in every port of the world. To our shame this is not true of the United States dollar, and the merchant who buys goods in China, Japan, India, Australia, or South America must pay for them by sterling exchange on London, which is good everywhere. This is mainly owing to want of confidence in our monetary system, which is likely to undergo some radical change at any session of Congress. The permanent establishment of our money unit on a gold basis would be an effectual remedy for the evil, and confidence would be everywhere established.

NOT GOLD ENOUGH.

The claim that there is not gold enough for the business transactions of the country is a great mistake. Where there is confidence enough there is gold enough, and no amount of silver will suffice for the lack of confidence. Two or three twists of the British lion's tail and a foolish threat of paying our debts with silver, will give wings to a few millions of gold, which flies away to London, taking the place of our own securities. Then we employ J. P. Morgan & Co. to coax it back again, and pay the freight both ways. With the confidence inspired by a sound monetary system all the gold required will come to us for the asking, so long as our rates of interest exceed the rates in England.

Business is paralyzed and stagnant at all points in the United States, not from want of money or other facilities, but for want of confidence. Every business man is distrustful and anxious for the immediate future, therefore he folds his hands and waits.

We cannot look for a permanent revival of business until this question is settled and the United States adopts a monetary system equal to the best. Our present system is demonstrably the worst in the world. If we take to our grocer five dollars in silver and five dollars in gold, he will take either or both in exchange for his goods, although one metal is worth only half as much as the other. He does this because the United States Government *makes good the difference and pays it out of the public treasury.* Hundreds of millions have been paid out in this way for the purpose of holding up silver to parity with gold regardless of its commercial value. All this has been done for the protection of the silver producer alone, and to the detriment of every other industry. It is time that the silver industry should seek its own markets and stop drawing gold from the United States treasury for protection.

If there is too much silver, stop the production; if there is not too much, then let those who have it sell to those who want it, just as all other commercial products are sold, and no one will interfere. An immense amount of silver will always be required for fractional coins and the payment of small debts even under a single gold standard; and these are said to embrace the greatest amount of all human transactions where money actually passes from hand to hand.

By the United States treasury reports we find that about 87 per cent. of our imports and more than 92 per cent. of our exports are from and to countries where gold is the single standard. It is evident, therefore, that any other standard would be inconvenient, confusing, and detrimental to trade.

Under free coinage acts over a period of eighty years only $8,000,000 were called for by the people of the United States. Under forced coinage acts $215,000,000 were coined in eight years, but few went into circulation. Nobody will export them because our legal tender acts cannot go with them. Nobody will melt them because their bullion value is fifty per cent. less than the cost. To this extent, therefore, we will have to remain bimetallists, unless the government re-melts and sells the bullion at a loss of $107,000,000 more. Verily the experiment of holding up the price of silver against all other nations has been a very costly and instructive lesson to the people of the United States, and the time has come when silver must take its natural place with all other products, and its appropriate place with the moneys of the world, regardless of all other considerations.

BIMETALLISM.

Gold and silver cannot both be made a measure of the exchange values which applied to commodities constitutes the commerce of the world. The standard must be constant. It may be gold or it may be silver; but it cannot be both for the perfect reason that their relations to each other are not constant and cannot be made so even by international law.

If gold is the standard, the weight and fineness of the metal being established, then the money unit of one dollar becomes invariable; and a contract which has twenty days or twenty months or twenty years to run will be adjusted and satisfied without any appreciation or depreciation of the standard. But if it may be discharged and satisfied with dollars made either of gold or silver, then the payor may gain an enormous advantage by exercising his option, and the payee will lose what the payor gains. Such possibilities as this would prevent the making of any contracts or engagements which could be thus exposed, and the sale of long-time bonds, whether state, municipal, or corporate, would be impossible, and both public and private affairs would be sadly impeded and confused.

A piece of gold containing twenty-five and eight-tenths grains standard metal is made by law the unit of value, and is called a dollar. Possessing two of these pieces, with or without the mint stamp, they will exchange each for the other on equal terms, and one as well as another for other commodities. There can be no such thing as rise or fall, appreciation or depreciation, shrinkage or expansion in the use or relation of these dollars to each other, nor in relation to the commodities whose value they measure in exchange. But when we erect another standard and make another dollar out of silver, calling four hundred and twelve and one-half grains of standard silver the exact equivalent of twenty-five and eight-tenths grains of gold, each dollar having the same function as the other and each being a legal standard of measure, we find ourselves in the midst of difficulties. The relation of one silver dollar to another silver dollar is constant, but the relation of a silver dollar to a gold dollar, and also to the commodities being measured, has changed materially; in fact, as much as fifty per cent. The result is that one or the other of these coins has ceased to be

a dollar; the gold coin is 150 cents, or the silver coin is only
50 cents, which is it? The gold partisan says that silver as
a value in exchange has fallen; the silver partisan says gold
has appreciated, — which is right? We go into the markets
and we find everywhere a surplus stock of silver for sale.
The great decline has created a suspicion as to its stability,
and it is so abundant that all fear it may go still lower;
therefore no one cares to take the risk of holding it. The
same testimony comes from all foreign markets; there is a
manifest over-production, and the supply is greater than the
demand. Silver is everywhere being dropped as a proper
measure because it is inconstant; the gold standard is everywhere being established because it is stable and constant.
We find that the mint values for gold show but trifling fluctuations anywhere, while the mints have very generally
ceased the coining of silver except for small change, and the
price at the mint is not in excess of the market for bullion.
The evidence, in fact, all points one way, and we are forced
to the conclusion that an over-production of silver has diminished the demand, and therefore four hundred and twelve
and one-half grains of standard silver are no longer one
dollar, but that twenty-five and eight-tenths grains of gold
still fits the standard, and is therefore our only standard
dollar, and it cannot rise above the standard in respect to
itself. There may be a great variation in respect to silver
and all other commodities, but none in respect to gold,
which is the standard measure by which all fluctuations are
determined, or it is not a *standard*.

All this proves conclusively that the stamp at the mint
certifies nothing but the actual weight and fineness of the
coin, and has nothing to do with values in exchange.

Holding silver to parity with gold when there is only half
a dollar's worth of silver in a silver dollar is like offering a
premium on clipped coins and counterfeits.

We deplore as much as any one can the condition of
things which checks the production of silver and affects in-
juriously a large industry in the mining states. We have
large interests there which must share in the general de-

pression; but there are fundamental principles which lie at the roots of our national prosperity the discarding of which will involve the whole country in disaster and ten times greater loss. Our present indebtedness *must be paid in gold;* and to this the good faith and honor of every good citizen in the United States is pledged, and it will be fulfilled.

Another evidence that it is silver which has declined, and not gold which has risen, is shown in the bad temper of the silver party and the means they employ to force upon the markets an artificial demand for a product for which there is no room. Let us not be deceived. The silver partisan, by the very means which he employs to force his goods upon an unwilling market, *confesses* that silver has lost its exchange power, and for that reason the price has fallen. In the bullion markets for gold there is no such disturbance, and the standard is maintained without artifice in any of its various phases.

Can the people of the United States restore the standard of measure to silver which it has lost, and by what means can it be done so that it will be permanent? This is the question which is now agitating the people, and from center to circumference the whole country seeks a complete answer to the question.

The double standard partizan says that it must be accomplished by legislation, and the commercial world must accept *nolens volens* the exchange values which are established by law. The single standard partisan says that the question must be governed by the natural force of economic laws, which cannot be regulated by statutes.

The double standard advocate claims that Congress has the power to fix the quantity of gold in a dollar and the quantity of silver in a dollar, and then to declare that the exchange value of these respective quantities is equal and that each shall be a legal tender for all amounts. The single standard advocate says that gold and silver are by nature both economic quantities, and that the exchange value will always be subject to variations under an economic law stated as follows: The value of silver to gold will *increase*—

First, by a decrease of the quantity ;
Second, by an increase of the demand.
So also the value will *decrease*—   } Macleod.
First, by an increase of the quantity;
Second, by a decrease of the demand.

He claims also that the means for the *increase* of one and the *decrease* of the other cannot be made permanent by any statutory act which can be passed by any power or convention of powers.

He claims also that while it is possible for legislative power to create a *standard* by fixing the unit of gold, thus making gold's value constant, and by which standard the increase or decrease of all other values must be measured, he denies that there can be two standards for the same measure, any more than there can be two specific gravities for the same substance. He admits that the standard unit may be fixed in silver, and that for economic purposes the use of silver by all nations could be made the universal measure. He denies the expediency of such a change, for the reason that ninety-five per cent. of all our foreign commercial transactions are with countries using the gold standard which will not change, and that such a change would be of great international embarrassment, very damaging to trade both foreign and domestic, and of no benefit to anybody other than the silver producer himself, and of no permanent benefit to him, for sooner or later continued production will overwhelm the demand, the standard will be disregarded, and chaos will prevail. The economic law will then assert itself, and the statute become obsolete.

To this the silver advocate replies :—"The fifty-cent silver dollar was caused by the demonetization of silver. By reason of the *appreciation of gold* the farmer's products have fallen in value. If other things which the farmer wants have fallen also, he does not get the benefit of it because he sells at wholesale and buys at retail. What we want is a dollar which will hold its parity with the property which that dollar is to buy."—[Bryan's speeches.

Economist replies:—

Speaking of dollars as measures of value, there are no fifty-cent dollars in the United States, for the government has maintained their parity with gold and has paid the cost. A silver dollar will therefore buy just as much wheat as a gold dollar. It is a blunder, therefore, to say that the farmer's products have fallen because gold has appreciated; gold *has not appreciated*, and the farmer can get gold dollars for his wheat just as well as silver dollars, if he wants them. It does not seem probable that under free coinage the farmer will be any more likely to buy at wholesale than before. What is meant by 'a dollar which will hold its *parity with property*,' I do not understand. There is no such thing as parity with property, and there is no standard for parity other than gold. Parity with wheat, cotton, and dried codfish would be nonsense, and yet dried codfish was once used as money. The farmer knows very well that the price of silver and gold bullion in the United States can have nothing to do with the price of wheat, for that is determined by the supply in Liverpool and Russia and the Argentine; when the crops are large the price is small. On the other hand, he would have the miner believe that multiplying dollars under a free coinage act is going to put up the price of silver dollars and pull down the price of gold, thus reversing the law of supply and demand. The farmer wants to sell his product and buy dollars; the owner of dollars wants to sell his dollars and buy wheat; what object then has the farmer in putting up the price of dollars? The price of wheat is controlled by conditions beyond the seas.

The silver advocate continues:—

"A double standard and free coinage will make money abundant and easy to get, so that the western farmer can pay off his mortgage to the eastern money grabber and get out of debt, rather than lose his farm by process of foreclosure. 'A young man buys a farm, pays $1,000 down and gives a mortgage for the other thousand. Money *rises in value* until it is worth *twice as much* as it was when the man gave the mortgage, so that it takes twice as much wheat to pay the interest, twice as much to pay the taxes, and twice as much to pay the debt. The value of the land has gone down, and the farm is no longer security even for the $1,000 mortgage. The man who holds the mortgage gets the farm back, and is twice as well off as he was before. The young man who bought has lost everything, and must begin life again.' " — [Bryan's speeches.

Economist replies : —

From an economic standpoint here is a queer condition of things. *Money* has risen one hundred per cent. above its own standard, land has fallen over fifty per cent., and farm products and taxes *have not changed at all.* Such a condition of things cannot exist as has been here stated, for if the young man sells his farm product for *money* under the precise condition stated, then one-half of it will pay off just as much indebtedness as the whole would pay at the time he bought his farm. The illustration is a romance of the imagination, but not a fact in business life. When the silver advocate talks to the producer of silver, he wants free coinage and a full legal tender so as to *appreciate* the value of his silver money to parity with gold. When he talks to the farmer, he wants free coinage so as to make money cheap and abundant and thus *appreciate* the value of his product, but he says nothing about the legal tender. When he talks to the laborer, he wants free coinage, cheap money and enough of it, so as to *appreciate* the nominal wages paid for his toil, but he does not tell him that if his wages are paid in gold one-half the amount is better than the whole if paid in silver. Now he talks legal tender for the purpose of making the laborer believe that his silver has the same purchasing power as gold, and in that case he gets his wages doubled. If the legal tender clause is repealed then the silver dollar will only pass for its commercial value, fifty cents. Repeal the legal tender clause as to the gold dollar and it will still pass at its standard value, one hundred cents. The manifest object, then, of the full legal tender clause is to force the people of this country to accept fifty cents' worth of silver in place of one hundred cents' worth of gold. This is contrary to every principle of sound economics, contrary to every principle of commercial honesty, and it will never be done.

To say that money (meaning gold) is worth twice as

much at one time as it is at another, is simply darkening counsel by words without knowledge. In respect to itself gold cannot rise above its own standard. An ounce of standard gold in one man's hands will always exchange for an ounce of standard gold in another man's hands, an ounce of silver for another ounce of silver. The relation of an ounce of gold to an ounce of silver may change and so also the rise and fall of commodities can be determined by the relation to other commodities. When one commodity like gold or silver is separated from all other commodities and made the standard of measure then it can never rise or fall as a measure by the value of a single grain, for it has no other standard of comparison than its own quantity, and one quantity must always be equal to the same quantity of the same thing. If, however, for the sake of multiplying money we make a double standard and decree that sixteen ounces of silver shall be the equivalent of one ounce of gold, we immediately introduce an element of comparison ; the law of supply and demand asserts itself, and a question arises as to the true equation of the double standard ; there is an apparent difference in the measure ; has the gold standard lengthened ? or has the silver standard shortened ? Our inquiry is limited to the conditions which apply to the two measures, and we find that from 1860 to 1873 the silver measure was the longest by from two to four per cent.; in 1896 it is the shortest by 50 per cent. The gold standard has been treated as being constant : it did not lengthen to the silver standard when it was the longest, nor does it shrink to its smaller dimension when it is shortest, therefore, gold has not risen nor fallen but silver has reached such extremes of fluctuation, as to prove conclusively that a double standard cannot be maintained without a never-ending change of the commercial ratio. A scarcity of money may by increasing the rate of interest show an apparent increase in the demand for all kinds of money but it does not change the standard measure.

Bimetallism, then, means silver monometallism and nothing else.

The silver advocate says : —

" Every nation which goes to the gold standard increases the demand for gold, and every increase in the demand for gold raises the purchasing power of an ounce of gold and lowers the purchasing power of wheat and corn and other products of the farm. You enshrine gold as the one thing to be desired and all mankind pays tribute to the *golden calf*.

" While we want to get rid of the gold standard we must keep the thing which we don't want until aliens shall bring us the relief which we should achieve for ourselves. — [Bryan's speeches.

Economist replies : —

The purchasing power of wheat and cotton are not in any way affected by the question of a gold standard in foreign countries. Cheap labor in Russia, Egypt, and India can put these products in the warehouses of Liverpool cheaper than Iowa, Dakota, Minnesota, Illinois, or Kansas. It is *that* fact and not the kind of money used in payment which governs the price. India is on a silver basis, and practically so is the Argentine Republic, their crops are paid for in silver ; the English merchant first buys the money of the country with which he trades, and then pays it out for the commodities he wants. When wheat brought $1.35 per bushel in Dakota the price of gold and silver bullion in New York and London had nothing to do with it. The demand was great, crops were short, and the supply was relatively small, it was purely a question of supply and demand. And now when wheat is worth about one-third what it was then, it is still a question of supply and demand, and the ' rise of gold ' or ' fall of silver ' has nothing to do with it; the controlling factor is, how much have the competing countries got to sell and at what price will they sell it ?

If the legal tender clause should be repealed to-morrow and the outstanding certificates redeemed it would not put up the price of wheat, but it would take about twice as much coined silver to buy a bushel as it does now, and it would be worth no more to the farmer than the currency he gets now. It would not increase the purchasing power of his wheat,

3

even for another slice from the 'golden calf,' but it would send his children through the fires unto Moloch to get the last quotation for silver.

The leading advocates for a silver standard reject gold for the reason that its value has risen so high and so rapidly that the purchasing power of all commodities and products have been greatly reduced.

The advocates for a gold standard reject silver because it has fallen so low and so rapidly that double the quantity is required for the purchase of commodities that was needed before the decline, unless parity is maintained at government expense.

Only one of these propositions can be true in the main. The facts which bear upon the question are historical; but the conclusions are controlled in part by prejudice and in part by argument. The result is that different conclusions are drawn from the same state of facts, for the reason that a like cause does not invariably have the same effect; consequently the postulate assumed in one case will not apply to the other, for example: the sudden influx of gold between the years 1850 and 1875, greater in volume than the entire product for the previous 357 years, would quite naturally call for a marked decline in the exchange value, as the world's product for these twenty-five years was over *three thousand three hundred millions of dollars.* So far, however, from its causing a serious decline it was quickly sought for and absorbed by those far-seeing countries which desired to substitute a standard of gold for that of silver, and the result was that it crowded out an equal value in silver and took its place. This caused a decline in silver which was looked for in gold and gave an exception to the rule of excessive production, with a competent witness to the law of supply and demand.

A considerable proportion of that gold was from California, and if the United States had purchased it as a cover for gold certificates, this country would have been firmly established on a gold basis, its credit largely improved, and France, Germany, Belgium, and Holland would probably have been still on a silver basis. Keeping our gold would have improved our market for silver, of which we had enough and to spare, and fortified our national credit beyond the assaults and jibes of men.

Far-sighted Germany, having more wisdom, did just that thing. Seeing her opportunity to get the gold, she made a prompt sacrifice of her silver, but got nearly double what it would sell for now, *and made the grandest financial stroke of the century.* The United States did just the reverse,— bought silver and rashly agreed to maintain the certificates issued thereon at parity with gold. Permitting a re-issue of the same certificates brought the world's stock of silver within reach of a centrifugal pump demanding the price of parity, and unless it is stopped will bankrupt the government; for a single five-dollar certificate, rotated often enough, will exhaust the treasury of its gold. It was the worst financial blunder ever made, in striking contrast with the German policy, and we are paying dearly for it now.

It is not what you think or I think about the quality of the reserves which are the basis of our national credit. It is what the world thinks ; and if we have that which the world will take from us at any moment and at full face value, then our credit will be the best in the world, and we can get anything we want at the lowest price. But, on the other hand, if we have that which the world does not want and will not take except for the reason that we have nothing else to give, then the cost of keeping our credit on an equality with Great Britain, Germany, and Holland will be enormously greater than the difference in cost of filling our treasury with gold, which everybody wants, or filling it with silver, which has no market and nobody wants or can afford to keep for a rise.

The disturbance caused by the fall in silver has involved the country in losses more than double the value of all the silver in the vaults of the treasury. All of which would have been prevented if we had possessed financial wisdom enough to have backed our treasury certificates with gold instead of silver. That mistake cannot be too speedily repaired.

To the amazement of all other nations the United States

stands alone as the guarantor of a price for the world's silver, which shall be at parity with gold on the basis of 16 to 1. It is the most reckless and the most stupendous undertaking ever entered into by any nation, and imperils the property, the prosperity, and the social welfare of every family in the whole country. · Our national credit is already seriously impaired for this reason, and its resources are insufficient for the task which has been undertaken in support of a single industry, which has grown into such importance within the past twenty-five years.

LEGISLATION ABOUT DOLLARS.

In 1772 the United States dollar contained 377¼ grains of pure silver.

In 1785 the Federal Congress adopted the silver dollar as the money unit and fixed its quantity at 375.64 grains pure silver. The Spanish milled dollar contained 386⅞ grains pure.

The Act of 1792 fixed the weight at 371¼ grains pure and 416 grains standard, 44.75 grains being alloy.

The same act made the gold equivalent 24.73 grains pure, on the basis of 15 to 1. In 1809 the market value of gold was rated at 16½ times the weight of gold. Gold was then treated as a commodity, disappeared from circulation and was shipped abroad for foreign exchange. Silver became by its comparative cheapness the circulating medium, was everywhere recognized as the money unit. The ratio of 15 to 1 was the proposal of Alexander Hamilton and had the approval of Thomas Jefferson, who was then President, under the belief that both metals would circulate together under the ratio fixed by the act of 1792, but in this he was mistaken.

The mint was fully occupied in the coinage of silver, but none of the dollars came into circulation. It was then discovered that the bullion which came to the mint for coinage was principally in the shape of Spanish milled dollars, and that the new dollars were immediately shipped to the West Indies and to Mexico for exchange at par for Spanish dollars, and these were directly brought to the mint for re-coinage. Thus an honest Quaker banker in Philadelphia turned a handsome profit by the free use of the mint in coining our light dollars out of the heavy Spanish dollars, which trick coming to the knowledge of President Jefferson he issued an order stopping the coinage of dollars, and the Philadelphia banker had to quit that profitable business.

The coinage of the silver dollar was thus suspended until the year 1836. A special committee appointed in 1830 to consider the condition of the currency reported that since the establishment of the mint in 1794 about $37,000,000 had been coined, *four-fifths of which had been exported*, leaving only seven or eight millions in the United States after an expend-iture of nearly one million dollars, which Upton finds was "*the net result of free coinage of both metals for a period of fifty years.*"

Then came the war against the United States bank and the clamor for a change of the ratio from 15 to 1 to 16 to 1, which was approved by President Jackson, June 28, 1834.

The intention of the government was to restore gold to the currency and drive out the paper dollars issued by the United States bank. Silver was no longer thought of, and was completely demonetized. A bill was introduced to pro-vide for a limited coinage of subsidiary coins for change and small transactions, but it received no attention.

To promote the circulation of gold President Jackson directed that public officers should receive only specie in payment of public dues.

In 1846 the sub-treasury act provided that nothing but specie should be received by the government on any ac-count, and when received should be held until disbursed by public officers, and should not be deposited in any bank, hoping by this means to create a demand for hard money.

In 1852 the Senate passed a bill authorizing the Secre-tary of the Treasury to purchase silver bullion and to coin it into fractional pieces reduced by seven per cent. as to weight to be issued only at par in exchange for gold. This bill was introduced by the bimetallist, R. M. T. Hunter, who admitted that the only way to circulate both gold and silver was by the subordination of silver to gold. The double standard was admitted to be impracticable as one would always be subservient to the other. Mr. Dunham, who had charge of the bill, said:

"Gentlemen talk about a double standard of gold and silver as a thing that exists, but that we propose to change. We have had but a single standard for the last three or four years. That has been and is now gold. We propose to let it remain so, and adapt silver to it, and to regulate silver by it."

The bill became the law in February, 1853, and gave general satisfaction. Every one could get silver or gold either for labor or commodities, and the return to free coinage was not considered or desired by anybody. Fractional silver was abundant, and Upton says that for "the first time in the history of the country we had a true bimetallic currency, silver and gold circulating in harmony side by side," the market for silver being a little stronger than gold.

In April, 1870, the Secretary of the Treasury prepared and submitted a bill making new regulations in regard to the mint assay officers and coinage with a full report giving the reasons and the necessity for the changes recommended.

The report stated that under the existing and legal ratio between gold and silver, the silver dollar was at a premium of three and one-half per cent., but as the gold dollar was the unit of account no change of ratio was desirable, and the bill made no provision for further coinage of silver dollars as they could not be put in circulation when they were worth more for the melting pot than for money. On December 9th, the same year, the finance committee reported the bill to the Senate with amendments, and it was ordered to be printed. After a discussion which occupied two days it was passed and sent to the House.

On Jan. 13, 1871, the House ordered the bill to be printed and referred to the committee on coinage.

On February 25th the coinage committee reported the

bill with another amendment, when it was again ordered to
be printed and re-committed.

On March 9, 1871, the bill was again reported to the
House and ordered to be printed. On Jan. 9, 1872, Mr.
Kelley of Pennsylvania, chairman of the committee, recommended the passage of the bill, saying that the committee had considered the bill "with great deliberation, section
by section, line by line, and word by word."

After considerable discussion the bill was again re-committed, again reported, again printed, only to be again reported, again printed and made the special order for March
12, 1872, until disposed of. Then came a most exhaustive
discussion. Mr. Hooper of Massachusetts explained each
section of the bill, which explanation and argument occupied ten columns of the *Congressional Globe*, dwelling at great
length upon the reasons for discontinuing the coinage of
the silver dollar, the principal reason being that if put in
circulation the manufacturers of silver-ware could use them
at a profit over bullion, and they would immediately disappear.

Mr. Potter of New York contended that the legal tender
coin of the country should be of one metal instead of two,
and that should be of gold alone.

Mr. Kelley called attention to the fluctuating character of
two metals as a standard and urged that it would promote
domestic convenience by having a subsidiary coinage of
silver circulating in all parts of the country as a legal tender for small amounts.

On May 27, 1872, the bill passed the House, yeas 110,
nays 13.

The bill was prepared at the Treasury Department, and
amended by Congress, providing for the coinage of a silver
dollar weighing 384 grains, and making all the silver coins
a legal tender for $5 in any one payment instead of all sums
less than one dollar.

The bill was sent to the Senate and referred to Senate
committee on coinage and printed. Upon being reported
by that committee it was again printed. Further amend-

ments beings made by the Senate it was again printed with the amendments, and after a discussion which occupied nineteen columns in the *Congressional Globe* it passed the Senate.

The bill was then sent to the House, again printed and referred to a committee of conference, which committee reported the bill without further amendments and it became a law Feb. 12, 1873. The Senate amendments struck out the subsidiary dollar of 384 grains, and substituted the trade dollar of 420 grains for use in the China and Japan trade, but did not make it a legal tender.

This is the story of "*the crime of 1873*," and the so-called "*surreptitious passage*" of a bill, which was printed thirteen times by order of Congress, and the discussion and debates of which between April, 1870, and February, 1873, occupied no less than one hundred and forty-four columns in the *Congressional Globe*, printed and re-printed in every prominent newspaper in the country, and is now denounced by free silver orators, who have the cheek to say that they did not know what the bill meant or what it contained, although they voted for its final passage.

The claim of concealment and fraud, which these men set up regarding the passage of that bill, if it proves anything, proves that they were grossly neglectful of what was going on in the Congress where they had seats, and with whose acts they are charged with knowledge and responsibility. If they did not know what the bill contained, it is a shameful confession of neglect of public duty. If they did know, then their present claim is a still more shameful imposition upon the people whom they seek to deceive.

We have taken Upton's carefully studied account of the passage of this bill for an orderly presentation of the facts, which we have not seen disputed. [*Money in Politics*, pp. 201 *et seq.*]

The arguments made in Congress during the pendency of the bill against the propriety of coining silver dollars when they were worth more for the melting pot than for circulation, were unanswerable and unanswered. Under the condition of things which existed when the bill was enacted, the silver producer did not care whether his silver was made into dollars or forks and spoons, for it did not affect the price of his product. But when a few months after the bill became a law, the silver men's product began to fall, then they wanted full silver coinage to provide an outlet for their bullion and they began to denounce the law and all those who had a hand in its making, including themselves.

At no period in the world's history has there been any such great and continued decline in the silver product as we have seen since 1873, and that, and that only, is the cause of the present disturbance and the revolt of the silver producer.

The act of 1873 did not demonetize silver. It proscribed no coin from circulation. It sold neither coin nor bullion. It did not diminish its value by taking away its character as a legal tender. It *prevented any further purchases* except for subsidiary coins on government account which it was not profitable to send abroad, or melt for silver plate. For the same reason, the coining of silver dollars was suspended in 1806, but in 1873 no silver dollars were in circulation.

INTERNATIONAL CONFERENCE AND CONGRESS.

The first general convention was the result of discussions by the delegates to the Latin Union. France took the initiative, and the convention was held at Paris, June 17, 1867. The United States, Great Britain, France, Austria, Bavaria, Baden, Belgium, Denmark, Spain, Greece, Italy, the Netherlands, Portugal, Russia, Prussia, Sweden, Norway, Switzerland, Turkey, and Wurtemburg. Eight sessions were held and the conference was closed July 6, 1867. *All of the States represented declared in favor of a single gold standard.* The president, Dr. Parieu, in his valedictory speech, declared that the opinion of the conference "was in favor of a gold monometallic standard," and that was the limitation of the power conferred upon the convention, except its recommendations respecting a universal unit of money.

England, on the 18th of February, 1868, appointed a commission to consider the recommendations of the Paris conference. The commission sat from March 13th to July 8th, but arrived at nothing decisive except the rejection of the proposal to change the value of the pound sterling.

In France public opinion was strongly in favor of gold as the single standard, and so continued until the result of the war with Germany, which took the question of monetary legislation as an international question out of her hands.

Germany, however, did not neglect the opportunity of reforming her monetary system by a gold standard on the basis of 15.5 to 1. The legal tender act demonetized silver, and the silver coin was called in, put in the crucibles and sold as bullion, to the extent of two-thirds the circulation. In 1872 the Scandinavian States adopted gold in place of a silver standard. In May, 1876, the Netherlands changed from a silver to the gold standard.

Before and during the adjustment of these important changes the increasing production of silver in the United States so affected international exchanges that all nations found themselves in serious complications growing out of the rapid decline in silver.

The tribute payable by India to Great Britain, amounting to the gold value of about $80,000,000 per annum, was enormously increased when considered with the decreasing value of Indian rupees.

In March, 1876, Parliament appointed a commission to inquire into the causes for the depreciation in silver, but without power to suggest a remedy.

August 15, 1876, the United States Congress appointed a commission to inquire into the causes for the depreciation in silver and the feasibility of a bimetallic system as well as the resumption of specie payments. The majority, Jones, Bogy, Willard, Groesbeck, and Bland, reported a recommendation to remonetize silver, and to invite another international conference. The resulting act was known as the Bland bill. It authorized the coinage of the standard dollar and restored its legal tender character Feb. 28, 1878. On invitation from France the conference authorized by the same act met in Paris Aug. 10, 1878. The United States members recommended the free coinage of silver by a general agreement with full legal tender. Belgium, Switzerland, and Norway opposed this. England refused to modify her monetary system. Germany did not take part in the conference. France considered it useless to discuss an international ratio which was unattainable, and nothing was accomplished.

The situation was so serious that in May, 1879, Germany suspended the sales of silver.

On April 19, 1881, by request of the United States and on the invitation of France, a third international convention assembled in Paris. All of the European States, Canada, and India were represented, as well as the United States.

France, the United States, Austria, Italy, the Netherlands, and British India declared for bimetallism. Belgium, Switzerland, Greece, and the Scandinavian States declared against bimetallism. England and Germany declared that no change in their systems could be entertained, but in case of agreement among the nations, something might be done to increase the use of silver.

The convention closed July 8, 1881, by adjournment to April 12, 1882, to see what might be done by legislation in the interval. The convention, however was not again called together.

Agitation continued, and a bimetallic congress assembled at Cologne in October, 1882, but its resolutions did not have any influence on the Powers.

In the United States the proposed repeal of the compulsory coining clause in the Bland bill attracted general attention.

In England, Sept. 20, 1886, a royal commission was appointed to "inquire into the present changes in the relative values of the precious metals."

A divided report made no recommendation of any change, but suggested another international conference.

During the Paris Exhibition in 1889 a free International Congress was held, and on invitation of the committee 194 members attended ; but the congress closed without coming to any practical conclusion. The declination in the value of silver continued.

By invitation of the United States a conference was held in Brussels in 1892, the purpose being stated as follows :— " For the purpose of considering what measures, if any, could be taken to increase the use of silver in the currency systems of nations."

The convention met 26th November and delegates were present from Austria, Belgium, Hungary, Denmark, France, Germany, Great Britain, India, Greece, Italy, Mexico, The Netherlands, Norway, Portugal, Roumania, Russia, Sweden, Spain, Switzerland, Turkey, and the United States.

The usual discussion took place and a committee proposed that the European States will buy in each year 30,000,000 ounces of silver on condition that the United States continue to purchase 54,000,000 ounces per annum, and that free unlimited coinage be maintained in British India and Mexico. It was also proposed to withdraw the smaller gold coins and bank notes less than five dollars from circulation. This proposal was not agreed to. The attention of the congress was then turned to the bimetallic proposal of the United States.

The French delegate then stated clearly that he could not advise his government to open the mints to the free coinage of silver unless the monometallic states would do so; and that, as the question stood, the return to the free coinage of silver must be regarded as settled.

The United States stood alone in the proposal for bimetallism. India had already acted by requesting a committee of the British government to consider the proposal to close the Indian mints to the coinage of silver, *with a view to the adoption of a gold standard.*

HAS SILVER FALLEN IN VALUE?

It is a very singular circumstance that in view of all these international congresses, conventions, and conferences comprising the expert financiers and scientists of all nations to consider what proper means should be employed to arrest the decline in silver that there should be any one so blind to the fact, as to claim that it is not silver which has depreciated but gold which has appreciated.

It is instructive to read the arguments, prophecies, and declamations of senators and representatives on the passage of the coinage act of 1878 which was passed over the veto of the President. We were told then, as we are now, that the act of remonetizing silver would stop its decline, put it into circulation, make the rich contented, the poor happy, advance wages and prices, and bring us general prosperity; but it did nothing of the kind, and notwithstanding the purchases made by government, has continued its downward course.

Not a single speech made in favor of that bill will ever go into our school books as an example of forensic eloquence or statesmanship.

There was one, however, made against it by Senator Lamar of Mississippi, which will go down to posterity as a bright example of that honor and courage which abide, and sustain an honest soul under most trying circumstances.

The legislature of Mississippi instructed its senators to vote for the bill and also for the bill repealing the Resumption Act.

Senator Lamar, in justification of his refusal to obey these *instructions*, said :—

"Mr. President, between these instructions and my convictions there is a great gulf. I cannot pass it. . . . I have always endeavored to impress the belief that truth is better than falsehood, honesty better than policy, courage better than cowardice.

"To-day, my lessons confront me. To-day, I must be true or false, honest or cunning, faithful or unfaithful to my people. Even in this hour of their legislative displeasure and disapprobation I cannot vote as these resolutions direct, I cannot and will not shirk the responsibility which my position imposes. My duty, as I see it, I will do, and I will vote against this bill. . . Then it will be for them to determine if adherence to my honest convictions has disqualified me from representing them."

Those brave words will live, and that honest vote will be

cherished with pride in future years, as a model for that manliness and greatness of soul which refuses to lay official duty under the feet of a legislative power, which could condemn and punish, but could not dishonor.

The senator was right : and the bill proved to be an utter failure in all that was expected from it by its most ardent friends. It was in violation of every principle of economic law: and there was no power to clothe it with success.

The same reasons were urged for the passage of the act in 1890. Like causes led to its failure and repeal in 1893.

INDIA AS A FACTOR.

The important place which India occupies as a factor in the metallic currency systems of the world is not generally understood. She has a population three and one-half times larger than the United States, and has a very productive soil. The excess of her net imports of silver over exports for the year 1893 was $60,934,726. The excess for fifty-seven years previous (1836 to 1863) was $1,698.999,075. Professor Shaw tells us that during long periods India has been such a "sink" or receptacle of the world's metallic currencies as to be the recognized safety-valve of the nations, by providing an outlet for any sudden inflow of the precious metals, and thus has preserved the equilibrium when disaster to the currency system was imminent.

There had for a long time been a constant balance of trade in favor of India; but the steady fall in the value of silver from 1873 to 1893 was such as to turn her annual surplus into a large deficit, owing to her gold obligations to England.

The impending disaster was stayed by the large silver purchases made by the United States government, and it is now claimed that the only practical solution of India's difficulty is in the adoption of a gold standard. Such a course would naturally have the serious effect of precipitating a still further decline in silver, and might liberate such a vast volume of coin and bullion as to overwhelm all countries, and bring on a crisis which no country has the strength to stay or control.

For the United States to sit still and see other countries, one after another, firmly established on a gold basis, *remaining alone as the indorser and guarantor of the parity value of the world's gold and silver*, is only to invite a disaster which would be overwhelming and irreparable.

A free coinage act with unlimited tender, and a guarantee to maintain the parity of silver with gold "*in the markets and in the payment of debts*," on the basis of 16 to 1, or even 20 to 1, is the most reckless undertaking in the world, and no power or combination of powers will take the hazard.

It is plain to see how a full-fledged anarchist or an extreme socialist might advocate such a measure, for the result would be more destructive than dynamite, and society would have to be remodeled on some new plan.

A free coinage act on the basis indicated would immediately destroy the market for silver as a product of the United States, for the bullion of other countries would flow in an overwhelming stream to our mints, and at prices which would close every mine in the country and exhaust the treasury of its gold.

The scenes in the extra session of Congress in 1893 would be completely reversed, and all would hasten to repeal the act as they would fly to the extinguishment of a consuming fire.

So much for prophecy which is founded on the cupidity of mankind rather than any economic law; for all such questions would take on an exceptional phase, and, by a suspension of every well-known principle, wait for such reorganization and readjustment of human affairs as would mark a new era in both domestic and foreign affairs.

The cable has already advised us that "Englishmen are protesting against the minting of silver coins which cost but two shillings and sixpence per ounce, and selling it to the people for five shillings and sixpence." It is claimed that the government of Queen Victoria is pursuing the same disgraceful policy of the ministry of Queen Elizabeth who made sixty-two shillings out of twenty. As a silver-using people Englishmen protest against a "depreciated currency." The demand for a shilling's worth of silver in an English shilling may have its echo in the demand for a dollar's worth of silver in a silver dollar; that will go a long way in pacifying those who object to the fraud of a fifty-cent dollar. Give the people the full worth of their money and they will be peaceful and contented. There is no excuse which will satisfy either the English or American workman that half an ounce of silver is just as good as a whole one, because it would tire him less to lug it about. If the half ounce is only a token of the full ounce, and the mint must be paid for the whole in order to get the half, it would be quite safe to guarantee that the laborer would prefer the whole thing to the token, and would not complain of the weight.

If free coinage means that anybody can take one dollar's worth of silver to the mint and have free use of the machinery to stamp it as being two dollars, giving the silver owner instead of the government the benefit of the fraud, it is quite likely that the mints would be kept busy; but it would be far better if they were kept idle.

Laboring men and men of small means would derive no benefit from the free use of the mints, but the mine owners, the bullion dealers, and speculators generally, would have it all their own way, to the great detriment of the public.

FULL LEGAL TENDER.

Here lies the chief iniquity of the proposed act. Strip the cheap dollar of the fraudulent force which is given to it by these three words, and it will stand before the world on its honest merits. It will go to those who need and want it, instead of being forced at double price on those who do not want it.

The silver speculators and brokers could take contracts for the payment of other men's debts and mortgages, taking the same property thus improved by fifty per cent. as a security, and the mortgage indebtedness of the country could be liquidated by a *quasi* fifty per cent. bankrupt law, available to those abundantly able to pay, as well to as those who are not, thus legalizing the most stupendous system of fraud which has ever stained the annals of history.

The credit and the integrity of the government which would give sanction or opportunity to any such manipulation of its currency, would be a by-word and a hissing in the mouths of honest men the world over.

OVER-PRODUCTION.

When we speak of an over-production of gold or silver, we refer to three noticeable changes or effects produced by that cause, viz., the effect which an increasing supply has on the demand; the effect which such superabundant supply has on the fixed or legal ratio of one to the other; and the effect which such supply has on the exchange value for commodities and its relation to population.

It will be admitted without argument that the commodities which go into actual consumption have a demand which is in the main governed by population. The home market being supplied, the surplus flows into the channels of foreign commerce.

In American history the extraordinary production of the precious metals which is first noticed took place about the middle of the sixteenth century, the date for its beginning being fixed by the authorities at about 1545, and refers to the output from the mines of Potosi, Mexico, and Peru, being forty-five times more in silver than gold, and reducing the exchange value of silver for gold from thirty-five to forty per cent. in the course of the succeeding century. Notwithstanding the increased production of gold, which was subjected to the operation of the same economic law of supply and demand, the great preponderance of silver had the effect of changing the fixed ratio from 1 to 11 to 1 to 15 by the end of the century. The annual production not being consumed nor absorbed by a proportionate increase of population, was added to the pre-existing supply, and thus becoming an over-production, had the effect stated.

4

Professor Laughlin fixes the next noticeable period from 1780 to 1820, during which time, by reason of the increasing richness of the mines, especially those of Mexico, the product was much larger than for the entire century between 1545 and 1660. The effect, however, was not so marked, because of the much larger pre-existing mass to be also affected thereby. At this point Prof. Laughlin calls attention to the fact that the tables of prices do not disclose "any diminution in the purchasing power of gold"; for which reason he concludes that the change of relations was due to a further decline in silver.

The act of 1834 changed the ratio from 15 to 1 to 16 to 1, but diminished the weight of the gold coin as well, which reduced its value by six per cent. Under the operation of these changes gold came into circulation and silver retired.

The act of 1853, caused by the enormous influx of gold from California, placed gold in the same position which the act of 1834 gave to silver. Gold was the standard money of account, and no one concerned himself about ratios until the great decline in silver in 1876.

The world's gold product, 1851 to 1875, was $3,314,553,000
The silver product for same period was $1,395,125,000

This enormous gold product in twenty-five years, by reason of its great abundance crowded out silver, and by the increased demand for gold and the lessened demand for silver stayed the decline in gold and hastened the decline in silver. During the twelve years, 1852 to 1864, France alone imported $680,000,000 of gold and exported $345,000,000 of silver, showing that at that time there was an abundance of silver, and to spare. The production of silver in face of this circumstance was being rapidly increased. The silver product, which for the United States in 1860 was only $150,000, in 1873 was $35,750,000, and in 1892 $82,101,000.

From 1873 to 1895 it amounted to $1,214,751,000
From 1873 to 1895 the gold product was   .   .   . $830,660,000

These facts show an over-production sufficient to account for the continuous decline in silver.

COMPARED WITH WHEAT.

1866–95, average value wheat product per year,	$335,674,260
1866–95, average *decrease* in value per year,	3,194,487
1866–95, average price per bushel for period,	97.9
1866–95, average *fall in price* per bushel per year (cents),	5.6
Average price per bushel in 1866,	$2.19.6
Average price per bushel in 1895,	.50.9

SILVER PRODUCT COMPARED WITH POPULATION.

SILVER

1860–95, average product per year,	$37,983,361
1860–95, average yearly increase,	$1,997,250

POPULATION

1860–95, average population for period,	48,146,409
1860–95, average increase per year,	1,067,630
Percentage of average yearly increase in silver product to average production,	5.26 %
Percentage of average increase in population per year to average population for period,	2.21 %

SILVER

1873, value of silver per ounce,	$1.29
1895, value of silver per ounce,	.65
1873–95, ratio of value in '95 to value in '73,	50.4 %

WHEAT

1866–95, ratio of value in '95 to value in '66,	23.1 %

The increase in the production of silver has been more than double the increase in population. The decline in wheat has been more than three times the decline in silver; all of which demonstrates an overproduction of silver, which is the most important factor in accounting for the decline, except that the decline in wheat is owing to causes other than the decline in silver. It shows, also, that if gold is not absolutely stable as a measure of value it is incomparably more so than silver, which is liable in any year by excessive production to overwhelm the commercial world with remediless disaster.

The facts before us demonstrate that a bimetallic standard is utterly impossible; the chasm is too wide for legislation, and the preferences of mankind the world over cannot be changed by an act of Congress, nor by a congress of nations. We have reached a point where any increase in the production of gold will have the immediate effect of displacing silver, without loss of prestige or demand for the dominant metal.

The arts will be our future safety-valve for surplus silver, and the demand for subsidiary coinage will increase with the population.

CONCLUSION.

Taking the price of wheat and cotton in Liverpool for 1873 as a basis, we find a decline if applied to the crop of 1893 amounting to no less than (wheat) $213,018,400
Decline in cotton crop, 1893, 310,200,000

Total decline for two items, $523,218,400

If the prices realized in 1873 could have been realized in 1893-'94-'95, the western farmer and the southern planter would have been extremely happy.

We find also during the same period a decline of 50 per cent. in the price of silver, and we are told that this decline in silver is the cause of the decline in wheat and cotton, and that all we need to restore the price of wheat and cotton to the price of 1873 is to restore the price of silver.

The stubborn fact remains, however, that the decline in silver bullion has nothing to do with the decline in wheat and cotton; for during all this time the silver dollar has been kept at parity with gold at government expense, and if the total sales of wheat and cotton had been paid for in gold dollars or silver dollars, it would have made no difference to the farmer or the planter.

This shrinkage, then, of $523,218,000 must be accounted for in some other way. Looking for the cause, we find that Argentina in 1892 put in the same market 25,000,000 bushels of wheat; in 1893, 45,000,000 bushels; and in 1894,

75,000,000. We find, also, Egypt, India, and Russia in the same market with correspondingly large crops, and this enormous production forced down the price, and the silver crop had nothing to do with it. Silver coin in point of fact during all this time had the full benefit of friendly legislation and the full power of the government to maintain its parity with gold.

The truth is that we are in great danger of losing our foreign markets by means of foreign competition, and we cannot meet that competition by any change in our monetary standard. Great Britain will buy her wheat and cotton where she can buy it the cheapest. With the Liverpool merchant it is a question of business and not of sentiment. He wants to know what our dollar weighs, and the inscription, "In God we trust," is not taken as evidence of commercial value.

The monsoons of the Indian Ocean and cheap foreign labor have more to do with the price of wheat in Liverpool than has the price of silver in the United States.

How can we protect our foreign markets against foreign labor is a question which cannot be answered by the means employed to protect our home markets against the same force.

The orators who are so fond of proclaiming our independence of foreign powers should address themselves to the duty of finding the means by which these same foreigners can be forced to pay us double the present price for our own products. Cheap bread stuffs is the universal cry of mankind, and the country which can meet that requirement best will command the market and fix the price.

We cannot legislate double price for our silver product any more than we can for our farm products. It is simply a question of supply and demand. The nations of the whole earth are our competitors, and we cannot overcome it by putting up the price of our commodities, much less that of silver, of which they have much more for sale even now than we have.

Prof. Laughlin in his "Gold and Prices since 1873,"

gives many interesting facts which are instructive, as they show that for the past twenty-five years food products have increased faster than the population, and this fact has to be considered in accounting for the decline in prices as measured by gold, as well as the decreased cost of production and delivery.

In 1870 acres planted to wheat in United States, . .	88,000,000
In 1884 acres planted to wheat in United States, . .	157,000,000
In 1870 India planted acres	18,000,000
In 1884 India planted acres . .	25,000,000
In 1870 Europe planted acres . . .	440,000,000
In 1884 Europe planted acres . . .	482,000,000
In 1869-70 European imports of grain, value	$409,000,000
In 1879 European imports of grain, value . .	$817,000,000
In 1873 Rio coffee shipped to New York, tons	68,863
In 1886 Rio coffee shipped to New York, tons	189,319

The general fall in prices has been rashly attributed to appreciation in gold, when the causes to be found are entirely distinct from any influence whatever by the precious metals. Increased cheapness in production and distribution has brought an over-supply, which has had its natural effect in the markets of the world. Coincidences are too frequently magnified into original causes, and time is required to dispel the illusion.

The fact therefore that the decline in wheat, cotton, corn, sugar, and silver, were contemporaneous events, is no more conclusive that the decline of one has caused the decline of the other, than is the large reduction of tonnage dues at the Suez canal, the cause of a decline in silver, while it is a direct cause for the decline of wheat in Chicago.

The causes for the general decline in prices are complex, world-wide, and various. It follows, therefore, if this be true, that neither the reduction of gold to a parity with silver, nor the uplifting of silver to a parity with gold by international law, will necessarily advance the price of American wheat and cotton.

APPENDIX.

TABLE I.

Commercial Ratio of Silver to Gold each Year since 1687.

[NOTE.— From 1687 to 1832 the ratios are taken from Dr. A. Soetbeer ; from 1833 to 1879 from Pixley and Abell's tables, and from 1879 to 1896 from daily cablegrams from London to the Bureau of the Mint.]

Year.	Ratio.	Year.	Ratio.	Year.	Ratio.	Year.	Ratio.	Year.	Ratio.	Year.	Ratio.
1687	14.94	1722	15.17	1757	14.87	1792	15.17	1827	15.74	1862	15.35
1688	14.94	1723	15.20	1758	14.85	1793	15.00	1828	15.78	1863	15.37
1689	15.02	1724	15.11	1759	14.15	1794	15.37	1829	15.78	1864	15.37
1690	15.02	1725	15.11	1760	14.14	1795	15.55	1830	15.82	1865	15.44
1691	14.98	1726	15.15	1761	14.54	1796	15.65	1831	15.72	1866	15.43
1692	14.92	1727	15.24	1762	15.27	1797	15.41	1832	15.73	1867	15.57
1693	14.83	1728	15.11	1763	14.99	1798	15.59	1833	15.93	1868	15.59
1694	14.87	1729	14.92	1764	14.70	1799	15.74	1834	15.73	1869	15.60
1695	15.02	1730	14.81	1765	14.83	1800	15.68	1835	15.80	1870	15.57
1696	15.00	1731	14.94	1766	14.80	1801	15.46	1836	15.72	1871	15.57
1697	15.20	1732	15.09	1767	14.85	1802	15.26	1837	15.83	1872	15.63
1698	15.07	1733	15.18	1768	14.80	1803	15.41	1838	15.85	1873	15.92
1699	14.94	1734	15.39	1769	14.72	1804	15.41	1839	15.62	1874	16.17
1700	14.81	1735	15.41	1770	14.62	1805	15.79	1840	15.62	1875	16.59
1701	15.07	1736	15.18	1771	14.66	1806	15.52	1841	15.70	1876	17.88
1702	15.52	1737	15.02	1772	14.52	1807	15.43	1842	15.87	1877	17.22
1703	15.17	1738	14.91	1773	14.62	1808	16.08	1843	15.93	1878	17.94
1704	15.22	1739	14.91	1774	14.62	1809	15.96	1844	15.85	1879	18.40
1705	15.11	1740	14.94	1775	14.72	1810	15.77	1845	15.92	1880	18.05
1706	15.27	1741	14.92	1776	14.55	1811	15.53	1846	15.90	1881	18.16
1707	15.44	1742	14.85	1777	14.54	1812	16.11	1847	15.80	1882	18.19
1708	15.41	1743	14.85	1778	14.68	1813	16.25	1848	15.85	1883	18.64
1709	15.31	1744	14.87	1779	14.80	1814	15.04	1849	15.78	1884	18.57
1710	15.22	1745	14.98	1780	14.72	1815	15.26	1850	15.70	1885	19.41
1711	15.29	1746	15.13	1781	14.78	1816	15.28	1851	15.46	1886	20.78
1712	15.31	1747	15.26	1782	14.42	1817	15.11	1852	15.59	1887	21.13
1713	15.24	1748	15.11	1783	14.48	1818	15.35	1853	15.33	1888	21.99
1714	15.13	1749	14.80	1784	14.70	1819	15.33	1854	15.33	1889	22.10
1715	15.11	1750	14.55	1785	14.92	1820	15.62	1855	15.38	1890	19.76
1716	15.09	1751	14.39	1786	14.96	1821	15.95	1856	15.38	1891	20.92
1717	15.13	1752	14.54	1787	14.92	1822	15.80	1857	15.27	1892	23.72
1718	15.11	1753	14.54	1788	14.65	1823	15.84	1858	15.38	1893	26.49
1719	15.09	1754	14.48	1789	14.75	1824	15.82	1859	15.19	1894	32.56
1720	15.04	1755	14.68	1790	15.04	1825	15.70	1860	15.29	1895	31.00
1721	15.05	1756	14.94	1791	15.05	1826	15.76	1861	15.50	1896 6 mo.	30.32

TABLE II.

The following table exhibits the value of the pure silver in a silver dollar, reckoned at the commercial price of silver bullion from $0.50 to $1.2929 (parity), per ounce fine.

Price of silver per fine ounce.	Value of pure silver in a silver dollar.	Price of silver per fine ounce.	Value of pure silver in a silver dollar.	Price of silver per fine ounce.	Value of pure silver in a silver dollar.	Price of silver per fine ounce.	Value of pure silver in a silver dollar.
$0.50	$0.387	$0.71	$0.549	$0.92	$0.712	$1.13	$0.874
.51	.394	.72	.557	.93	.719	1.14	.882
.51	.402	.73	.565	.94	.727	1.15	.889
.53	.410	.74	.572	.95	.735	1.16	.897
.54	.418	.75	.580	.96	.742	1.17	.905
.55	.425	.76	.588	.97	.750	1.18	.913
.56	.433	.77	.596	.98	.758	1.19	.920
.57	.441	.78	.603	.99	.766	1.20	.928
.58	.449	.79	.611	1.00	.773	1.21	.936
.59	.456	.80	.619	1.01	.781	1.22	.944
.60	.464	.81	.626	1.02	.789	1.23	.951
.61	.472	.82	.634	1.03	.797	1.24	.959
.62	.480	.83	.642	1.04	.804	1.25	.967
.63	.487	.84	.650	1.05	.812	1.26	.975
.64	.495	.85	.657	1.06	.820	1.27	.982
.65	.503	.86	.665	1.07	.828	1.28	.990
.66	.510	.87	.673	1.08	.835	1.29	.998
.67	.518	.88	.681	1.09	.843	*1.2929	1.000
.68	.526	.89	.688	1.10	.851	*Parity.	
.69	.534	.90	.696	1.11	.859		
.70	.541	.91	.704	1.12	.866		

TABLE III.

The total redemptions of notes in gold and the exports of that metal during each fiscal year *since the resumption of specie payments* have been as follows:

Fiscal Year.	United States notes.	Treasury notes of 1890.	Total.	Exports of gold.
1879	$7,976,698		$7,976,698	$4,587,614
1880	3,780,638		3,780,638	3,639,025
1881	271,750		271,750	2,565,132
1882	40,000		40,000	32,587,880
1883	75,000		75,000	11,600,888
1884	590,000		590,000	41,081,957
1885	2,222,000		2,222,000	8,477,892
1886	6,863,699		6,863,699	42,952,191
1887	4,224,073		4,224,073	9,701,187
1888	692,596		692,596	18,376,234
1889	730,143		730,143	59,952,285
1890	732,386		732,386	17,274,491
1891	5,986,070		5,986,070	86,362,654
1892	5,352,243	$3,773,600	9,125,843	50,195,327
1893	55,319,125	46,781,220	102,100,345	108,680,844
1894	68,242,408	16,599,742	84,842,150	76,978,061
1895	109,783,800	7,570,398	117,354,198	66,131,183
1896	153,307,591	5,348,365	158,655,956	112,309,186
Total	$426,190,220	$80,073,325	$506,263,545	$753,453,981

TABLE IV.

The following tables exhibit the amount and cost of silver bullion purchased each year under the acts of February 28, 1878, and July 14, 1890, the average price paid, and the bullion value of the standard silver dollar:

Amount, Cost, Average Price, and Bullion value of the Silver Dollar of Silver purchased under act of February 28, 1878.

Fiscal Year.	Fine ounces.	Cost.	Average price per fine ounce.	Bullion value of a silverd llar.
1878, . .	10,809,350.58	$13,023,268.96	$1.2048	$0 9318
1879, . .	19,248,086.09	21,593,642.99	1.1218	.8676
1880, . .	22,057,862.64	25,235,081.53	1.1440	.8848
1881, . .	19,709,227.11	22,327,874.75	1.1328	.8761
1882, . .	21,190,200.87	24,054,480 47	1.1351	.8779
1883, . .	22,889,241.24	25,577,327.58	1.1174	.8642
1884, . .	21,922,951.52	24,378,383.91	1.1120	.8600
1885, . .	21,791,171.61	23,747,460.25	1.0897	.8428
1886, . .	22,690,652.94	23,448,960.01	1.0334	.7992
1887, . .	26,490,008.04	25,988,020.46	.9810	.7587
1888, . .	25,386,125.32	24,237,553.20	.9547	.7384
1889, . .	26,468,861.03	24,717,853.81	.9338	.7222
1890, . .	27,820,900.05	26,899,326.33	.9668	.7477
1891, . .	2,797,379.52	3,049,426.46	1.0901	.8431
Total, .	291,272,018.56	308,279,260.71	1.0583	.8185

TABLE V.

Amount, Cost, Average Price, and Bullion Value of the Silver Dollar of Silver purchased under act of July 14, 1890.

Fiscal Year.	Fine ounces.	Cost.	Average Price per fine ounce.	Bullion value of a silverdollar.
1891, .	48,393,113.05	$50,577,498.44	$1.0451	$0.8083
1892, .	54,355,748.10	51,106,607.96	.9402	.7271
1893, .	54,008,162.60	45,531,374.53	.8430	.6520
1894, .	11,917,658.78	8,715,521.32	.7313	.5656
Total, .	168,674,682.53	155,931,002.25	.9244	.7150

Total cost purchases under both acts, $464,210,262.96.

TABLE VI.

[Senate Mis. Doc. No. 36, Fifty-third Congress, first session.]

Production of Gold and Silver in the World, 1792–1892.

Calendar years.	Gold.	Silver (coining value).
1792–1800, .	$106,407,000	$328,860,000
1801–1810, .	118,152,000	371,667,000
1811–1820, .	76,063,000	224,786,000
1821–1830, .	94,479,000	191,444,000
1831–1840, .	134,841,000	247,930,000
1841–1848, .	291,144,000	259,520,000
1849, . .	27,100,000	39,000,000
1850, . .	44,450,000	39,000,000
1851, . .	67,600,000	45,000,000
1852, . .	132,750,000	40,600,000
1853, . .	155,450,000	40,600,000
1854, . .	127,450,000	40,600,000
1855, . .	135,075,000	40,600,000
1856, . .	147,600,000	40,650,000
1857, . .	133,275,000	40,650,000
1858, . .	124,650,000	40,650,000
1859, . .	124,850,000	40,750,000
1860, . .	119,250,000	40,800,000
1861, . .	113,800,000	44,700,000
1862, . .	107,750,000	45,200,000
1863, . .	106,950,000	49,200,000
1864, . .	113,000,000	51,700,000
1865, . .	120,200,000	51,950,000
1866, . .	121,100,000	50,750,000
1867, . .	104,025,000	54,225,000
1868, . .	109,725,000	50,225,000
1869, . .	106,225,000	47,500,000
1870, . .	106,850,000	51,575,000
1871, . .	107,000,000	61,050,000
1872, . .	99,600,000	65,250,000
1873, . .	96,200,000	81,800,000
1874, . .	99,750,000	71,500,000
1875, . .	97,500,000	80,500,000
1876, . .	103,700,000	87,600,000
1877, . .	114,000,000	81,000,000
1878, . .	119,000,000	95,000,000
1879, . .	109,000,000	96,000,000
1880, . .	106,500,000	96,700,000
1881, . .	103,000,000	102,000,000
1882, . .	102,000,000	111,800,000
1883, . .	95,400,000	115,300,000
1884, . .	101,700,000	105,500,000
1885, . .	108,400,000	118,500,000
1886, . .	106,000,000	120,600,000
1887, . .	105,775,000	124,281,000
1888, . .	110,197,000	140,706,000
1889, . .	123,489,000	162,159,000
1890, . .	113,150,000	172,235,000
1891, . .	120,519,000	186,733,000
1892, . .	130,817,000	196,105,000
Total, . .	5,633,908,000	5,077,961,000

TABLE VII.

The silver product is given at its commercial value, reckoned at the average market price of silver each year, as well as its coining value in United States dollars.

Product of gold and silver from mines in the United States, 1873-1895.

Calendar year.	GOLD.		SILVER.		
	Fine ounces.	Value.	Fine ounces.	Commercial value.	Coining value.
1873,	1,741,500	$36,000,000	27,650,000	$35,890,000	$35,750,000
1874,	1,620,563	33,500,000	28,849,000	36,869,000	37,300,000
1875,	1,615,725	33,400,000	24,518,000	30,549,000	31,700,000
1876,	1,930,162	39,900,000	30,009,000	34,690,000	38,800,000
1877,	2,268,788	46,900,000	30,783,000	36,970,000	39,800,000
1878,	2,476,800	51,200,000	34,960,000	40,270,000	45,200,000
1879,	1,881,787	38,900,000	31,550,000	35,430,000	40,800,000
1880,	1,741,500	36,000,000	30,320,000	34,720,000	39,200,000
1881,	1,678,612	34,700,000	33,260,000	37,850,000	43,000,000
1882,	1,572,187	32,500,000	36,200,000	41,120,000	46,800,000
1883,	1,451,250	30,000,000	35,730,000	39,660,000	46,200,000
1884,	1,489,950	30,800,000	37,800,000	42,070,000	48,800,000
1885,	1,538,325	31,800,000	39,910,000	42,500,000	51,600,000
1886,	1,693,125	35,000,000	39,440,000	39,230,000	51,000,000
1887,	1,596,375	33,000,000	41,200,000	40,410,000	53,350,000
1888,	1,604,841	33,175,000	45,780,000	43,020,000	59,195,000
1889,	1,587,000	32,800,000	50,000,000	46,750,000	64,646,000
1890,	1,588,880	32,845,000	54,500,000	57,225,000	70,465,000
1891,	1,604,840	33,175,000	58,330,000	57,630,000	75,417,000
1892,	1,596,375	33,000,000	63,500,000	55,563,000	82,101,000
1893,	1,739,323	35,955,000	60,000,000	46,800,000	77,576,000
1894,	1,910,813	39,500,000	49,500,000	31,422,000	64,000,000
1895,	2,254,760	46,610,000	55,727,000	36,445,000	72,051,000
Total, .	40,183,481	$830,660,000	939,576,000	$943,083,000	$1,214,751,000

TABLE VIII.

Product of gold and silver in the United States from 1792 to 1844, and annually since.

[The estimate for 1792-1873 is by R. W. Raymond, Commissioner, and since by Director of the Mint.]

Year.	Ratio.	Gold.	Silver.	Total.
April 2, 1792-July 31, 1834, ...		$14,000,000	Insignificant.	$14,000,000
July 31, 1834-Dec. 31, 1844, ...		7,500,000	$250,000	7,750,000
1845, ...	15.92	1,008,327	50,000	1,058,327
1846, ...	15.90	1,139,357	50,000	1,189,357
1847, ...	15.80	889,085	50,000	939,085
1848, ...	15.85	10,000,000	50,000	10,050,000
1849, ...	15.78	40,000,000	50,000	40,050,000
1850, ...	15.70	50,000,000	50,000	50,050,000
1851, ...	15.46	55,000,000	50,000	55,050,000
1852, ...	15.40	60,000,000	50,000	60,050,000
1853, ...	15.33	65,000,000	50,000	65,050,000
1854, ...	15.33	60,000,000	50,000	60,050,000
1855, ...	15.38	55,000,000	50,000	55,050,000
1856, ...	15.38	55,000,000	50,000	55,050,000
1857, ...	15.27	55,000,000	50,000	55,050,000
1858, ...	15.38	50,000,000	500,000	50,500,000
1859, ...	15.19	50,000,000	100,000	50,100,000
1860, ...	15.29	46,000,000	150,000	46,150,000
1861, ...	15.50	43,000,000	2,000,000	45,000,000
1862, ...	15.35	39,200,000	4,500,000	43,700,000
1863, ...	15.37	40,000,000	8,500,000	48,500,000
1864, ...	15.37	46,100,000	11,000,000	57,100,000
1865, ...	15.44	53,225,000	11,250,000	64,475,000
1866, ...	15.43	53,500,000	10,000,000	63,500,000
1867, ...	15.57	51,725,000	13,500,000	65,225,000
1868, ...	15.59	48,000,000	12,000,000	60,000,000
1869, ...	15.60	49,500,000	12,000,000	61,500,000
1870, ...	15.57	50,000,000	16,000,000	66,000,000
1871, ...	15.57	43,500,000	23,000,000	66,500,000
1872, ...	15.63	36,000,000	28,750,000	64,750,000
1873, ...	15.92	36,000,000	35,750,000	71,750,000
1874, ...	16.17	33,500,000	37,300,000	70,800,000
1875, ...	16.59	33,400,000	31,700,000	65,100,000
1876, ...	17.88	39,900,000	38,800,000	78,700,000
1877, ...	17.22	46,900,000	39,800,000	86,700,000
1878, ...	17.94	51,200,000	45,200,000	96,400,000
1879, ...	18.40	38,900,000	40,800,000	79,700,000
1880, ...	18.05	36,000,000	39,200,000	75,200,000
1881, ...	18.16	34,700,000	43,000,000	77,700,000
1882, ...	18.19	32,500,000	46,800,000	79,300,000
1883, ...	18.64	30,000,000	46,200,000	76,200,000
1884, ...	18.57	30,800,000	48,800,000	79,600,000
1885, ...	19.41	31,800,000	51,600,000	83,400,000
1886, ...	20.78	35,000,000	51,000,000	86,000,000
1887, ...	21.13	33,000,000	53,350,000	86,350,000
1888, ...	21.99	33,175,000	59,195,000	92,370,000
1889, ...	22.10	32,800,000	64,646,000	97,446,000
1890, ...	19.76	32,845,000	70,465,000	103,310,000
1891, ...	20.92	33,175,000	75,417,000	108,592,000
1892, ...	23.72	33,000,000	82,101,000	115,101,000
1893, ...	26.49	35,955,000	77,576,000	113,531,000
1894, ...	32.56	39,500,000	64,000,000	103,500,000
1895, ...	31.60	46,610,000	72,051,000	118,661,000
1896, (6 mos.)	30.32			
Total, . . .		$2,059,946,769	$1,368,901,000	$3,428,847,769

TABLE IX.

Statement of the coin and paper circulation of the United States from 1860 to 1896, inclusive, with amount of circulation per capita.

Year.	Coin in United States, including bullion in Treasury.	Paper money in United States.	Total money.	Coin, bullion, and paper money in Treasury.	Circulation.	Population.	Money in United States per capita.	Circulation per capita.
1860	$235,000,000	$207,102,477	$442,102,477	$6,695,225	$435,407,252	31,443,321	$14.06	$13.85
1861	250,000,000	202,005,767	452,005,767	3,600,000	448,405,767	32,064,000	14.09	13.98
1862	25,000,000	333,452,079	358,452,079	23,754,135	334,697,744	32,704,000	10.96	10.23
1863	25,000,000	649,867,283	674,867,283	79,473,245	595,394,038	33,365,000	20.23	17.84
1864	25,000,000	680,588,007	705,588,067	35,946,589	669,641,478	34,046,000	20.72	19.67
1865	25,000,000	745,129,755	770,129,755	55,426,760	714,702,995	34,748,000	22.16	20.57
1866	25,000,000	729,327,254	754,327,254	80,839,010	673,488,244	35,469,000	21.27	18.99
1867	25,000,000	703,200,612	728,200,612	66,208,543	661,992,069	36,211,000	20.11	18.28
1868	25,000,000	691,553,578	716,553,578	36,449,017	680,104,561	36,973,000	19.38	18.39
1869	25,000,000	690,351,180	715,351,180	50,898,289	664,452,891	37,756,000	18.95	17.60
1870	25,000,000	697,868,461	722,868,461	47,655,667	675,212,794	38,558,371	18.73	17.50
1871	25,000,000	716,812,174	741,812,174	25,923,169	715,889,005	39,555,000	18.75	18.10
1872	25,000,000	737,721,565	762,721,565	24,412,016	738,309,549	40,596,000	18.70	18.19
1873	25,000,000	749,445,610	774,445,610	22,563,801	751,881,809	41,677,000	18.58	18.04
1874	25,000,000	781,024,781	806,024,781	29,941,750	776,083,031	42,796,000	18.83	18.13
1875	25,000,000	773,273,509	798,273,509	44,171,562	754,101,947	43,951,000	18.16	17.16
1876	52,418,734	738,264,550	790,683,284	63,073,896	727,609,358	45,137,000	17.52	16.12
1877	65,837,506	697,216,341	763,053,847	40,738,964	722,314,883	46,353,000	16.46	15.58
1878	102,047,907	689,205,669	791,253,576	62,120,942	729,132,634	47,538,000	16.62	15.32
1879	357,268,178	694,253,363	1,051,521,541	232,889,748	818,631,793	48,866,000	21.52	16.75
1880	494,363,884	711,565,313	1,205,929,197	232,546,969	973,382,228	50,155,783	24.04	19.41
1881	647,868,682	758,673,141	1,406,541,823	292,303,704	1,114,238,119	51,316,000	27.41	21.71
1882	703,974,839	776,566,880	1,480,531,719	306,241,300	1,174,290,419	52,495,000	28.20	22.37
1883	769,749,048	873,749,768	1,643,489,816	413,184,120	1,230,305,696	53,693,000	30.60	22.91
1884	801,068,939	904,385,250	1,705,454,189	461,528,220	1,243,925,969	54,911,000	31.06	22.65
1885	872,175,823	945,482,513	1,817,658,336	525,089,721	1,292,568,615	56,148,000	32.37	23.02
1886	903,027,304	905,532,390	1,808,559,694	555,859,169	1,252,700,525	57,404,000	31.50	21.82
1887	1,007,513,901	892,928,771	1,900,442,672	582,903,529	1,317,539,143	58,680,000	32.39	22.45
1888	1,092,391,690	970,564,259	2,062,955,949	690,785,079	1,372,170,870	59,974,000	34.39	22.88
1889	1,100,612,434	974,738,277	2,075,350,711	694,989,062	1,380,361,649	61,289,000	33.86	22.52
1890	1,152,471,638	991,754,521	2,144,226,159	714,974,889	1,429,251,270	62,622,250	34.24	22.82
1891	1,163,185,054	1,032,039,021	2,195,224,075	697,783,368	1,497,440,707	63,975,000	34.31	23.41
1892	1,232,854,331	1,139,745,170	2,372,599,501	771,252,314	1,601,347,187	65,520,000	36.21	24.44
1893	1,213,413,584	1,109,988,808	2,323,402,392	726,701,147	1,596,701,245	66,946,000	34.70	23.85
1894	1,251,543,158	1,168,891,623	2,420,434,781	759,626,073	1,660,808,708	68,397,000	35.39	24.28
1895	1,260,987,506	1,137,619,914	2,398,607,420	796,638,947	1,601,968,473	69,878,000	34.33	22.93
1896	1,225,618,792	1,120,012,536	2,345,631,328	839,000,302	1,506,631,026	71,390,000	32.86	21.10

NOTE 1. — Specie payments were suspended from January 1, 1862, to January 1, 1879. During the greater part of that period gold and silver coins were not in circulation except on the Pacific Coast, where, it is estimated, the specie circulation was generally about $25,000,000. This estimated amount is the only coin included in the above statement from 1862 to 1875, inclusive.

NOTE 2. — In 1876 subsidiary silver again came into use, and is included in this statement, beginning with that year.

NOTE 3. — The coinage of standard silver dollars began in 1878 under the act of February 28, 1878.

NOTE 4. — Specie payments were resumed January 1, 1879, and all gold and silver coins, as well as gold and silver bullion in the Treasury, are included in this statement from and after that date.

NOTE 5. — This table represents the circulation of the United States as shown by the revised statements of the Treasury Department for June 30 of each of the years specified.

EXPLANATION OF THE TABLES.

Table 1 shows the changes in the commercial ratio of Silver to Gold from 1687 to 1896 inclusive, 210 years. In 1687 14.94 ounces of silver was the equivalent of one ounce of gold. In 1896 30.32 ounces of silver is required to purchase one ounce of gold. Has the purchasing power of silver *decreased*, or the exchange value of gold *increased?*

TABLE III.

This table shows that when specie payments were resumed on the 1st of January, 1879, public confidence was so great in the outstanding paper issues of the United States, that, although the treasury was provided with $135,000,000 of gold, only $7,976,698 were presented for redemption during the balance of the fiscal year. It shows also, that the silver fright in 1896 sent in no less than $158,655,956 for redemption in about the same time.

TABLES IV AND V

Show the cost of silver purchased under the Acts of 1878 and 1890, $464,210,262.96 and which to-day is not worth one-half the cost.

TABLE VI

Shows the world's total product of gold and silver for one hundred years, 1792 to 1892, the difference being only $5,559,470.

TABLE VII

Product of gold and silver from the mines in the United States from 1873 to 1895.

TABLE VIII

Product of gold and silver in the United States from 1792 to 1896, showing the annual increase in volume.

TABLE IX

Shows the amount and kind of currency and bullion in the United States, the amount in circulation per capita, and the amount in reserve.

[From Treasury Documents.]
SUMMARY OF MONETARY EVENTS SINCE 1786.

1786.— Establishment of the double standard in the United States with a ratio of 1 to 15.25; that is, on the basis of 123.134 grains of fine gold for the half eagle, or $5 piece, and 375.64 grains of fine silver for the dollar, without any actual coinage.

1792.— Adoption of the ratio of 1 to 15 and establishment of a mint with free and gratuitous coinage in the United States; the silver dollar equal to 371¼ grains fine, the eagle to 247½ grains fine.

1803.— Establishment of the double standard in France on the basis of the ratio of 1 to 15½, notwithstanding the fact that the market ratio was then about 1 to 15.

1810.—Introduction of the silver standard in Russia on the basis of the ruble of 17.99 grams of fine silver, followed in 1871 by the coinage of imperials, or gold pieces of 5 rubles, of 5.998 grams; therefore, with a ratio of 1 to 15. This ratio was changed by the increase of the imperial to 5 rubles 15 copecks, and later to 1 to 15.45.

1815.— Great depreciation of paper money in England, reaching 26½ per cent. in May. Cost of gold, £5 6s., and of silver, 71½d. per ounce standard. In December the loss was only 6 per cent.; gold at this period was quoted at £4 3s., and silver at 64d.

1816.—Abolition of the double standard in England, which had had as its basis the ratio of 1 to 15.21, and adoption of the gold standard on the basis of the pound sterling at 7.322 grams fine in weight.

Coinage of divisional money at the rate of 66d. per ounce. Extreme prices, £4 2s. for gold and 64d. for silver; in January, £3 18s. 6d., and 59¼ in December

1816.— Substitution for the ratio of 1 to 15.5 in Holland, established by a rather confused coinage, of the ratio of 1 to 15⅔.

1819.-- Abolition of forced currency in England. Price of gold £3 17s. 10½d., and of silver, 62d.* per ounce in October, against £4 1s. 6d. and 67d. in February.

1832.— Introduction of the monetary system of France into Belgium, with a decree providing for the coinage of pieces of 20 and 40 francs, which, however, were not stamped. Silver, 59¼d.

---

* The price of silver given hereafter represents the average rate per ounce standard — that is, the mean between the highest price and the lowest price quoted during the year.

1834.— Substitution of the ratio of 1 to 16 for that of 1 to 15 in the United States by reducing the weight of the eagle, ten-dollar gold-piece, from 270 grains to 258 grains.

In 1837 the fineness of the United States gold coins was raised from .899225 to .900, and the silver coins from .8924 to .900, giving a ratio of 1 to 15.988 and fixing the standard weight of the silver Collar at 412½ grains. Silver .59-15/16d.

1836.— Introduction of the company rupee, a piece of silver weighing 165 grains fine, in India in place of the sicca rupee. Creation of a trade coin — the mohur, or piece of 15 rupees — containing 165 grains of fine gold. Silver, 59⅛d.

1844.— Introduction of the double standard in Turkey, with the ratio of 1 to 15.10. Silver 59½d.

1847.— Abolition of the double standard in Holland by the introduction of the silver standard on the basis of a 1-florin piece 0.945 grams fine, the coinage of which had already been decreed in 1839. Silver, 59⅛d.

1847.— Discovery of the gold mines of California.

1848.— Coinage in Belgium of pieces of 10 and 25 francs in gold, a shade too light. These pieces were demonetized and withdrawn from circulation in 1884. Silver, 59½d.

1848.— Replacing the ratio of 1 to 16 in Spain, which had been in force since 1786, by that of 1 to 15.77.

1850.— Introduction of the French monetary system in Switzerland without any actual coinage of gold pieces. Silver, 60₁/₆d.

1851.— Discovery of the gold mines of Australia.

1853.— Lowering of the weight of silver pieces of less value than $1 to the extent of 7 per cent. in the United States, and limitation of their legal tender power to $5. Silver, 61½d.

1853.— Maximum of the production of gold reached in California, when it amounted to $65,000,000.

1854.— Introduction of the gold standard in Portugal on the basis of the crown of 16.257 grams fine. Before this period the country had the silver standard, with a rather large circulation of gold coins stamped on the basis of 1 to 15½ in 1835 and 1 to 16½ in 1847. Silver, 61½d.

1854.— Modification of the ratio of 1 to 15.77 in Spain by raising it to 1 to 15.48, and by lowering the piaster from 23.49 grams to 23.36 grams fine.

1854.— Introduction of the silver standard, as it existed in the mother country, in Java, in place of the ideal Javanese money, and coinage of colonial silver pieces.

1857.— Conclusion of a monetary treaty between Austria and the German States, in accordance with which 1 pound of fine silver (one-half a kilogram) was stamped into 30 thalers or 52½ florins of south Germany, or 45 Austrian florins, resulting in 1 thaler equaling 1¾ German florins or 1½ Austrian florins. Silver, 61¾ d.

1861.— Law decreeing the coinage of gold pieces of 10 and 20 francs exactly equal to French coins of the same denomination in Belgium. Silver, 61¾ d.

1862.— Adoption of the French monetary system by Italy. Silver, 61 7⁄6 d.

1865.— Formation of the Latin Union between France, Belgium, Switzerland, and Italy on the basis of a ratio of 1 to 15½. Silver, 61 1⁄6 d.

1868.— Adoption of the French monetary system by Roumania with the exclusion of the 5-franc silver piece, which was, however, stamped in 1881 and 1883. Silver, 60½ d.

1868.— Admission of Greece into the Latin Union. The definite and universal introduction of the French monetary system into the country was effected only in 1883.

1868.— Adoption of the French monetary system, with the peseta or franc as the unit, by Spain. The coinage of gold alphonses d'or of 25 pesetas was made only in 1876.

1871.— Replacing of the silver standard in Germany by the gold standard. Coinage in 1873 of gold pieces of 5, 10, and 20 mark pieces, the latter weighing 7.168 grams fine. Silver, 60½ d.

1871.— Establishment of the double standard in Japan with the ratio of 1 to 16.17 by the coinage of the gold yen of 1.667 grams and of the silver yen of 26.956 grams, both with a fineness of 0.900.

1873.— Increase of the intrinsic value of the subsidiary coins of the United States. Replacing of the double standard by the gold standard. Reduction of the cost of coinage of gold to one-fifth per cent., the total abolition of which charge was decreed in 1875. Creation of a trade dollar of 420 grains with a fineness of 0.900. Silver, 59¼ d.

1873.— Suspension of the coinage of 5-franc pieces in Belgium.

1873.— Limitation of the coinage of 5-francs on individual account in France.

1873.— Suspension of the coinage of silver in Holland.

1873.— Formation of the Scandinavian Monetary Union. Replacing of the silver standard in Denmark, Sweden, and Norway by that of gold on the basis of the krone. Coinage of pieces of 10 and 20 kroner, the later weighing 8.961 grams, with a fineness of 0 900.

1874.— Introduction of the system of contingents for the coinage of 5-franc silver pieces in the Latin Union. Silver, 58$\frac{5}{16}$d.

1875.— Suspension of the coinage of silver on individual account in Italy. Silver, 56⅞d.

1875.— Suspension of the coinage of silver on account of the Dutch colonies.

1875.— Introduction of the double standard in Holland on the basis of the ratio of 1 to 15.62 by the creation of a gold piece of 10 florins, weighing 5.048 grams fine, with the maintenance of the suspension of the coinage of silver.

1876.— Great fluctuations in the price of silver, which declined to 46¾d., representing the ratio of 1 to 20.172, in July. Recovery, in December, to 58½d. Average price, 52¾d.

1877.— Coinage of 5-franc silver pieces by Spain continued later, notwithstanding the decline of silver in the market. Silver, 54¾d.

1877.— Replacing of the double standard in Finland by that of gold on the basis of the mark or franc.

1878.— Act of United States Congress providing for the purchase, from time to time, of silver bullion, at the market price thereof, of not less than $2,000,000 worth per month as a minimum, nor more than $4,000,000 worth per month as a maximum, and its coinage as fast as purchased into silver dollars of 412½ grains. The coinage of silver on private account prohibited. Silver, 52$\frac{9}{16}$d.

1878.— Meeting of the first international monetary conference in Paris. Prolongation of the Latin Union to January 1, 1886.

1879.— Suspension of the sales of silver by Germany. Silver, 51¼d.

1881.— Second international monetary conference in Paris. Silver, 51$\frac{11}{16}$d.

1885.— Introduction of the double standard in Egypt. Silver, 48⅜d.

1885.— Prolongation of the Latin Union to January 1, 1891.

1886.— Great decline in the price of silver, which fell in August to 42d., representing a ratio of 1 to 22.5, and recovery, in December, to 46d. Modification of the coinage of gold and silver pieces in Russia. Silver, 45⅜d.

1887.— Retirement of the trade dollars by the Government of the United States in March. Demonetization of the Spanish piasters, known as Ferdinand Carolus, whose reimbursement at the rate of 5 pesetas ended on March 11. New decline of silver in March to 44d., representing the ratio of 1 to 21.43. Silver, 44⅝d.

1890.— United States — Repeal of the act of February 28, 1878, commonly known as Bland-Allison law, and substitution of authority for purchase of 4,500,000 fine ounces of silver each month to be paid for by issue of Treasury notes payable in coin. (Act of July 14, 1890.) Demonetization of 25,000,000 lei in pieces of 5 lei in Roumania in consequence of the introduction of the gold standard by the law of October 27th. Silver, 47¹¹⁄₁₆d.

1891.— Introduction of the French monetary system in Tunis on the basis of the gold standard. Coinage of national gold coins and bullion. Silver, 45¹⁄₁₆d.

1892.— Replacing of the silver standard in Austria-Hungary by that of gold by the law of August 2. Coinage of pieces of 20 crowns, containing 6.090 grams fine. The crown equals one-half florin. Meeting of the third international monetary conference at Brussels. Production of gold reaches its maximum, varying between 675,000,000 and 734,000,000 francs. Silver, 39¹³⁄₁₆d.

1893.— Suspension of the coinage of silver in British India and of French trade dollars on individual account. Panic in the silver market in July in London, when the price fell below 30d., representing the ratio of 1 to 31.43. Repeal of the purchasing clause of the act of July 14, 1890, by the Congress of the United States.

1895.— Adoption of the gold standard by Chile.

1895.— Russia decides to coin 100,000,000 gold rubles in 1896.

MONETARY SYSTEM OF THE UNITED STATES.

In 1786 the Congress of the Confederation chose as the monetary unit of the United States the dollar of 375.65 grains of pure silver. This unit had its origin in the Spanish piaster or milled dollar, which constituted the basis of the metallic circulation of the English colonies in America. It was never coined, there being at that time no mint in the United States.

The act of April 2, 1792, established the first monetary system of the United States. The bases of the system were : The gold dollar or unit, containing 24.75 grains of pure gold, and stamped in pieces of $10, $5, and $2½, denominated, respectively, eagles, half eagles, and quarter eagles ; the silver dollar or unit, containing 371.25 grains of pure silver. A mint was established. The coinage was unlimited and there was no mint charge. The ratio of gold to silver in coinage was 1 : 15. Both gold and silver were legal tender. The standard was double.

The act of 1793 undervalued gold, which was therefore exported. The act of June 28, 1834, was passed to remedy this, by changing the mint ratio between the metals to 1 : 16.002. This latter act fixed the weight of the gold dollar at 25.8 grains, but lowered the fineness from 0.916⅔ to 0.899225. The fine weight of the gold dollar was thus reduced to 23.2 grains. The act of 1834 undervalued silver as that of 1792 had undervalued gold, and silver was attracted to Europe by the more favorable ratio of 1 : 15½. The act of January 18, 1837, was passed to make the fineness of the gold and silver coins uniform. The legal weight of the gold dollar was fixed at 25.8 grains, and its fine weight at 23.22 grains. The fineness was, therefore, changed by this act to 0.900 and the ratio to 1 : 15.988+.

Silver continued to be exported. The act of February 21, 1853, reduced the weight of the silver coins of a denomination less than $1, which the acts of 1792 and 1837 had made exactly proportional to the weight of the silver dollar, and provided that they should be legal tender to the amount of only $5. Under the acts of 1792 and 1837 they had been full legal tender. By the act of 1853 the legal weight of the half dollar was reduced to 192 grains and that of the other fractions of the dollar in proportion. The coinage of the fractional parts of the dollar was reserved to the Government.

The act of February 12, 1873, provided that the unit of value of the United States should be the gold dollar of the standard weight of 25.8 grains, and that there should be coined besides the following gold coins: A quarter eagle, or 2½ dollar piece; a 3-dollar piece; a half eagle, or 5-dollar piece; an eagle, or 10-dollar piece, and a double eagle, or 20-dollar piece, all of a standard weight proportional to that of the dollar piece. These coins were made legal tender in all payments at their nominal value when not below the standard weight and limit of tolerance provided in the act for the single piece, and when reduced in weight they should be legal tender at a valuation in proportion to their actual weight. The silver coins provided for by the act were a trade dollar, a half dollar, or 50-cent piece, a quarter dollar, and a 10-cent piece; the weight of the trade dollar to be 420 grains Troy; the half dollar 12½ grams; the quarter dollar and the dime, respectively, one-half and one-fifth of the weight of the half dollar. These silver coins were made legal tender at their nominal value for any amount not exceeding $5 in any one payment.

The charge for converting standard gold bullion into coin was fixed at one-fifth of 1 per cent. Owners of silver bullion were allowed to deposit it at any mint of the United States to be formed into bars or into trade dollars, and no deposit of silver for other coinage was to be received.

Section II of the joint resolution of July 22, 1876, recited that the trade dollar should not thereafter be legal tender, and that the Secretary of the Treasury should be authorized to limit the coinage of the same to an amount sufficient to meet the export demand for it. The act of March 3, 1887, retired the trade dollar and prohibited its coinage. That of September 26, 1890, discontinued the coinage of the 1-dollar and 3-dollar gold pieces.

The act of February 28, 1878, directed the coinage of silver dollars of the weight of 412½ grains troy, of standard silver, as provided in the act of January 18, 1837, and that such coins, with all standard silver dollars theretofore coined, should be legal tender at their nominal value for all debts and dues, public and private, except where otherwise expressly stipulated in the contract.

The Secretary of the Treasury was authorized and directed by the first section of the act to purchase from time to time silver bullion at the market price thereof, not less than $2,000,000 worth nor more than $4,000,000 worth per month, and to cause the same to be coined monthly, as fast as purchased, into such dollars. A subsequent act, that of July 14, 1890, enacted that the Secretary of the Treasury should purchase silver bullion to the aggregate amount of 4,500,000 ounces, or so much thereof as might be offered, each month, at the market price thereof, not exceeding $1 for 371.25 grains of pure silver, and to issue in payment thereof Treasury notes of the United States, such notes to be redeemable by the Government, on demand, in coin, and to be legal tender in payment of all debts, public and private, except where otherwise expressly stipulated in the contract. The act directed the Secretary of the Treasury to coin each month 2,000,000 ounces of the silver bullion purchased under the provisions of the act into standard silver dollars until the 1st day of July, 1891, and thereafter as much as might be necessary, to provide for the redemption of the Treasury notes issued under the act. The purchasing clause of the act of July 14, 1890, was repealed by the act of November 1, 1893.

The act of June 9, 1879, made the subsidiary silver coins of the United States legal tender to the amount of $10. The minor coins are legal tender to the amount of 25 cents.

www.ingramcontent.com/pod-product-compliance
Lightning Source LLC
Chambersburg PA
CBHW030027030726
47499CB00008B/3151